MEN~

compiled by
LEXUS

RICHARD DREW PUBLISHING
Glasgow

RICHARD DREW PUBLISHING LTD.
6 CLAIRMONT GARDENS
GLASGOW G3 7LW
SCOTLAND

First published 1990

ISBN 0 86267 268 6

Printed and bound in Great Britain by
Cox & Wyman Ltd.

CONTENTS

....

YOUR MENUMATE

gives you a comprehensive guide to eating out in 16 European countries:

Austria	Italy
Belgium	Norway
Denmark	Portugal
Finland	Spain
France	Sweden
Germany	Switzerland
Greece	Turkey
Holland	Yugoslavia

Each section has a concise introduction describing the main features and customs of eating out in the respective country, and includes notes on traditional national dishes and drinks, mealtimes, licensing and tipping.

This is followed by a section on useful phrases for **ORDERING** your meal and drinks, including a pronunciation guide with an underline to show which part of the word to stress. Just read the pronunciations as if they were English and you will communicate, although you might not sound like a native speaker.

SOME BASIC WORDS lists a selection of items that you may need to ask for, also with a pronunciation guide. The equivalent of 'a' and 'some' has been provided when this is the most appropriate form you are likely to use.

Last but by no means least, **UNDERSTANDING THE MENU** is a comprehensive menu reader consisting of an alphabetical listing of the main dishes, basic food items and drinks for each country. It also includes cooking methods and a number of regional specialities.

AUSTRIAN restaurants offer a good choice of standard meals as well as a variety of regional specialities, which are well worth trying. The same dish may appear under a different name depending on the region you are in. Special features of Austrian cuisine include **Mehlspeisen**, sweet dishes served as a main course, many of them made with yeast pastry and originating from Bohemia, which used to be part of Austria. They are all delicious but a little heavy on the untrained stomach. The most famous Austrian **Mehlspeise** is **Salzburger Nockerln**, a very light, sweet soufflé, usually served in vast quantities and a must if you visit Salzburg.

The **Kaffeehaus** is a main feature of every Austrian town. It is comfortable and civilized, and (especially in Vienna) daily newspapers are often provided for customers. In a **Kaffeehaus** you will find an abundance of cakes and gâteaux, which you can order with or without whipped cream ('**mit Sahne**' *[mit zahnuh]* or '**ohne Sahne**' *[ohnuh zahnuh]*), and many different kinds of coffee, all freshly made — try *them* with cream on top too! Other hot and cold drinks are also available, and you will often get a glass of water served with your coffee.

Both Austrian restaurants and cafés usually include VAT and service in their prices, but it is customary to round up the bill (for example 23ÖS to 30ÖS), and to say '**stimmt so**' *[shtimt zo]* which means 'keep the change'.

For some useful phrases on how to order your meal and for a more extensive guide to the menu, see the sections on German and German-Swiss Food.

5

....

UNDERSTANDING THE MENU

Apfelspalten/Apfelküchle apple fritters
Backhendl/Backhuhn chicken in
  breadcrumbs
Brandteigkrapfen profiteroles
Brathuhn roast chicken
Brettljause ploughman's lunch
Buchteln yeast dumplings filled with jam and
  served with custard
Dampfnudeln yeast dumplings
Faschingskrapfen doughnuts
Felchen whitefish
Fleischlaibchen meat balls
Fritattensuppe clear soup with thin slices of
  pancake
Germknödel yeast dumplings filled with thick
  plum jam and served with poppy seeds
Geröstel fried grated potato and onion with
  minced meat or bacon
Grießnockerlsuppe clear soup with semolina
  dumplings
Gugelhupf yeast cake with raisins and nuts,
  baked in a round mould with central funnel
Heidelbeernocken bilberry fritters
Hirschwurst venison sausage
Jägertee mulled wine with strong liquor and tea
Kässpätzle/Kasspatzeln home-made
  noodles made with strong local cheese
Kleiner Schwarzer small cup of black coffee
Leberknödelsuppe clear soup with liver
  dumplings
Marillenknödel apricots boiled in pastry and
  rolled in breadcrumbs
Melange/Milchkaffee large cup of white
  coffee
Mohnstollen yeast pastry
Moosbeernocken bilberry fritters
Palatschinken sweet or savoury stuffed
  pancakes

Powidltatschkerln small pastry bags filled with thick plum jam and rolled in breadcrumbs

Riebel fried semolina dish

Salzburger Nockerln sweet soufflé

Sachertorte chocolate cake

Scheiterhaufen bread and butter pudding

Schinkenfleckerl home-made noodles with ham

Schweinsstelze leg of pork

Steirisches Wurzelfleisch beef boiled and served with root vegetables

Tafelspitz boiled beef

Tirolerknödel bread and bacon dumplings

Topfen curd cheese

Topfenstrudel like apple strudel, but filled with a sweet mixture of curd cheese and raisins

Zwetschkenknödel plums boiled in pastry and rolled in breadcrumbs

BELGIUM is a small country with a big gastronomic reputation.

The French tend to make jokes about the Belgians, a large number of which feature the ubiquitous **frites** — as 'French fries' were not invented in France at all, but in Belgium. Even today every town or village has its roadside **friterie**, a mobile stall selling French fries, sausages, delicious rissoles, doughnuts etc.

Although largely influenced by France, Belgian cuisine has its own distinctive character, often due to the regional ingredients used. Many savoury dishes are cooked with beer — which is not surprising since there are almost 500 local brews to choose from — including several still brewed in monasteries by monks and others flavoured with cherries or raspberries.

In the Ardennes, game features strongly in delicious pâtés, stews and pastries. Along the coast you can enjoy sole, monkfish (**lotte**), mussels and the delicious, tiny grey shrimps which are still sometimes caught in nets dragged by sturdy Brabant horses as they wade through the surf.

Belgians are proud of their culinary tradition — and very aware of it. In Britain, the number one topic of conversation may be the weather, in Belgium it is certainly the latest, most fashionable restaurant and its specialities. But you can also eat divinely well in the small, local **bistrot**.

One last word about languages. Six Belgians out of ten speak Flemish as their mother tongue. Four out of ten speak French. The north and west of the country (Flanders) is mainly Flemish-speaking and the south and east (Wallonia), mainly French-speaking. Brussels is bilingual. Before you order, check which language the menu is written in. A little effort to communicate in Flemish, where appropriate, will win you smiles of approval.

The key phrases you use to order in restaurants will be the same you would use in Paris or Amsterdam (Flemish is a dialect — and most Flemings would insist, a purer form — of Dutch). So see also the French and Dutch sections. But beware of tricky variations in French, e.g. breakfast is not **petit déjeuner** but **déjeuner**, lunch is not **déjeuner** but **dîner** and dinner is not **dîner** but **souper**.

FLEMISH SPECIALITIES

asperges op s'Vlaams Flemish white
  asparagus, served with chopped boiled egg and
  melted butter

bloedworst delicious black pudding *(each
  butcher has his own recipe)*

boerenplattekaas fresh, soft cheese

Brabantse faisant pheasant with endives

garnaalen croquetten shrimp croquettes,
  deep-fried

gevulde tomaten tomatoes stuffed with North
  Sea shrimps and mayonnaise

Gentse waterzooi: waterzooi is halfway
  between a broth and a stew and is a meal in
  itself — in Ghent they make it with chicken,
  fresh vegetables and cream

kaas fondue deep-fried cheese croquettes

kip-kap brawn

konijn op s'en Vlaams rabbit hotpot,
  simmered with beer

krentebrood raisin bread

mossel frites mussels, usually cooked in wine
  with vegetable stock and sometimes cream,
  and served with a side-dish of French fries

paling in t'groen literally 'green eels',
  prepared with a mixture of herbs, including
  sorrel

pannekoeken Belgian pancakes, wafer thin
  and mouth watering

peperkiek spicy cake

potjesvlees pâté of veal, bacon and rabbit

pralines those famous Belgian chocolates,
  often filled with fresh cream or liqueurs

rollmops marinated herring

rijstaart rice pudding in pastry

smoutebollen hot doughnuts

Ternatse witloof endives with potatoes and
  bacon

vlaaien Flemish custard tart

Vlaamse cabeljauw cod baked in beer
Vlaamse carbonade beef, gently stewed in beer and onions — mmmmh!
waffels met suiker en slagroom waffles with sugar and whipped cream

SPECIALITIES FROM WALLONIA

baisers de Malmédy kind of meringue
bigorneaux winkles
boudin de foie 'Lefgot' black pudding made with pig's liver
boudin Liégeois white pudding with herbs
boudins noirs et blancs black and white pudding
côtelettes 'à l'berdouille' chops with a thick sauce of tarragon and shallots
crottes de Baudet small, strong cheeses
écrevisses à la Liégeoise crayfish with sloe berries
escavèche de Chimay marinated freshwater fish
filet américain steak tartare — spiced and seasoned to your taste
gâteau Ardennais cake made with potatoes
gaufres de Liège thick waffles containing sugar lumps
jambon d'Ardennes smoked ham
lapin aux pruneaux rabbit cooked with prunes
marcassin young wild boar, generally marinated, then roasted
pistolets breakfast rolls, crispy outside, soft inside
rognons de veau à la Liégeoise kidneys grilled with sloe berries
saucissons d'Ardennes spicy, salami-type sausage

....

soupe de la Lesse fish soup made with pike
tarte de curé apple pie *(curate's pie)*
tarte au sucre brun tart made with egg and
  demerara sugar
Trappistes an order of monks, well known for
  their beers and cheeses, e.g. Maredsous,
  Chimay etc.

ALTHOUGH foreign-type eating establishments are by no means uncommon in Denmark, most restaurants and cafés serve traditional Danish food. The standard of cooking is normally high, but do not expect great imagination in the use of spices and herbs. The culinary glory of the Danish table is undoubtedly the open dark-ryebread sandwiches and the cold buffet. The sandwiches (**smørrebrød**, *smurruh-brurth*), made up and garnished in advance, can be had virtually everywhere. The cold buffet is confined to good cafés, restaurants, hotels and country inns, and there are two types: 1. **platte** *[pladduh]*, which consists of various cold courses (fish, meats, cheese) served at your table; 2. **koldt bord** *[cult bor]*, which is a buffet proper in the sense that you help yourself to as much as you like from a central table. If you are not used to a Danish cold buffet, a piece of advice: your first excursion to the table should be in pursuit of fish only (unless you do not like fish). Do not pile your plate high with just anything that takes your fancy. Remember that you can return to the buffet table as often as you like, and that it is the custom to change your plate and cutlery after the fish course.

As for alcoholic drinks, it is customary to drink wine with hot food although many Danes prefer beer (**øl** pronounced '*url*'), which is almost invariably lager, called **pilsner**. This is also what accompanies sandwiches or a cold buffet (never wine), and it is worth knowing that Danish low-alcohol lagers are very palatable (ask for **a lys pilsner**, pronouncing **lys** '*lewss*'). During a cold buffet it is normal to have a **snaps** or two. A **snaps** is a small glass of ice-cold aquavit (a potato-based liquor), from which you do not sip without toasting your companions with the word 'skål' *[skawl].*

Country inns are very popular. They normally serve good wholesome food, and compete with each other in the quality of their cold buffets called **kroplatte** (**kro** being the Danish word for a country inn). These establishments also serve traditional and delicious home-made pastries, cakes and fresh cream gâteaux, which Danes are particularly fond of consuming in large quantities on Sunday afternoons. If you feel like afternoon coffee (or tea) Danish style, but do not wish to leave town, go to a **konditori** *[kondiddoree].*

Service and VAT (**MOMS**) are always included in your bill and you are not expected to leave a tip.

ORDERING

excuse me!
undskyld!
[awnskewl]

can I order please?
jeg vil gerne bestille
[yɪ vil gairnuh bistilluh]

one . . ./two . . .
en . . ./to . . .
[ain . . ./toh . . .]

that's for me/him
det er til mig/ham
[day air til mɪ/ham]

can you bring me another red wine/beer?
må jeg bede om en rødvin/øl mere?
[maw yı bay om in ruˍrthveen/url maˍiruh]

could I have the bill please?
må jeg bede om regningen?
[maw yı bay om rıˍningen]

The waiter/waitress will say '**værs' go**' when
he/she brings you something, and may also say
'**velbekomme**', which means 'enjoy your meal'.
Your answer to either is '**tak**' ('thank you').
When calling a waiter, say '**tjener**' *[chaˍynor]*,
which means 'waiter'; when calling a waitress,
say '**frøken**' *[fruˍggen]*, which means 'Miss'.

SOME BASIC WORDS

beer en øl *[in url]*
bottle en flaske *[in flaˍskuh]*
brandy en cognac *[in koˍnyak]*
bread brød *[brurth]*
coffee kaffe *[kaˍffuh]*
cup en kop *[kop]*
dry tør *[tur]*
fork en gaffel *[in gaˍffel]*
fruit juice en juice *[in juice]*
glass et glass *[it glass]*
gin and tonic en gin og tonic *[in gin aw toˍnic]*
half-bottle en halv flaske *[in hahl flaˍskuh]*
hot chocolate en varm kakao *[in vahm kakaˍ-oh]*
ice is *[eess]*
knife en kniv *[in k-neev]*
lager en pilsner *[in peeˍlsnor]*
lemonade en citronvand *[in citroˍhn-van]*
milk mælk *[melk]*

....

mineral water *(still)* not usually found in
  Denmark
mineral water *(fizzy)* en danskvand *[in
  dansk-van]*
napkin en serviet *[in sairvee-yet]*
orange juice en orangejuice *[in ohrangshe-
  juice]*
pepper peber *[piwwor]*
red wine rødvin *[rurth-veen]*
rosé rosé
salt salt *[sahlt]*
spoon en ske *[skay]*
sugar sukker *[sawggor]*
sweet sød *[surth]*
tea te *[tay]*
water vand *[van]*
whisky en whisky *[in whisky]*
white wine hvidvin *[veeth-veen]*

UNDERSTANDING THE MENU

agurkesalat sliced pickled cucumber
akvavit aquavit *(a potato-based liquor)*
ananas pineapple
and duck
appelsin ... orange ...
asparges asparagus
bagt(e) baked
benløse fugle beef or veal olives
biksemad med spejlæg fried potatoes with
  chopped meat and a fried egg
blomkål cauliflower
blomkålsgratin cauliflower soufflé
blomme ... plum ...
boller 1. meat and flour dumplings in broth;
  2. buns
boller i karry meat balls in curry sauce
boller i selleri meat balls in celeriac sauce

brasede kartofler sautéed potatoes
brisler sweetbread
brombær blackberries
brunede kartofler glazed potatoes *(fried or baked with sugar)*
brunkål med flæsk savoury browned cabbage with belly of pork
brød bread
budding blancmange
bækforel trout
bøf med løg minced beef with onions
bøf ta(r)tar finely chopped raw fillet of beef with a raw egg yolk, capers and raw onion
bønner beans
cacaolikør chocolate liqueur
champignons mushrooms
champignonstuvning creamed mushrooms
citron lemon
citronfromage lemon mousse
citronvand lemonade
dagens middag today's dinner
dagens ret dish of the day
dampet, dampkogt steamed
dansk bøf minced beef steak
danskvand mineral water
due pigeon
dyrekølle haunch of venison
dyreryg saddle of venison
dyrlægens natmad pâté, salt beef, meat jelly and raw onion on rye bread
engelsk bøf steak and onions
farseret stuffed
fasan pheasant
fersken peach
ferskrøget laks smoked salmon
fiskefilet med remoulade fish fillet with mustard sauce
fiskefrikadeller fish rissoles
flûte dinner roll
flæsk belly of pork or bacon

flæskekarbonade minced pork steak
flæskesteg med rødkål roast pork with
  sweet-and-sour red cabbage
flæskeæggekage bacon omelette
fløde cream
fløderand vanilla mousse
flødeskum whipped cream
forel trout
forloren hare meat loaf
forloren skildpadde sherry-flavoured stew
  with meat and fish balls, and hardboiled eggs
forretter starters
forårsrulle spring roll
franskbrød white bread
frikadeller pork rissoles
friturestegt deep-fried
fromage mousse
frugt(er) fruit
fyldt(e) filled, stuffed
gelé jelly
gemyse vegetables
glaseret, glaserede glazed *(fried or baked
  with sugar)*
gravad laks marinated salmon
grønkål curly kale
grønlangkål creamed curly kale
grønne bønner green beans
grøn salat green salad
grøn(t)sager vegetables
grønærter 1. green peas; 2. creamed peas
gule ærter med flæsk yellow split-pea soup
  with belly of pork
gulerødder carrots
gås goose
hachis minced beef in gravy
hakkebøf med løg minced beef steak with
  onions
halvsød medium sweet
halvtør medium dry
hamburgerryg smoked pork loin

haresteg roast hare
hellefisk flounder
helleflynder halibut
helstegt roasted as a joint
hindbær ... raspberry ...
hjemmelavet home-made
hjerter i flødesovs heart in a creamy white
  sauce
hofdessert meringue with chocolate-flavoured
  whipped cream
hummer ... lobster ...
hummerhaler lobster tails
hvidkål white cabbage
hvidkålsrulle stuffed cabbage
hvidkålssuppe cabbage soup
hvidløg garlic
hvidløgssmør garlic butter
hvidvin white wine
hvidvinsgelé white-wine jelly
højreb saddle of beef
høns chicken
hønsefrikassé creamy chicken stew
hønsekødsuppe chicken broth with dumplings
  and vegetables
is ice cream
isanretning ice cream dessert
jordbær ... strawberry ...
kaffe coffee
kage(r) cake(s)
kalkun turkey
kalv(ekød) veal
kalvefrikassé creamy veal stew
kanin rabbit
karamelrand caramel custard
karbonade minced pork steak
karrysalat chopped egg in curry dressing
kartofler potatoes
kartoffelmos mashed potatoes
kastanie ... chestnut ...
kiks crackers, biscuits

kirsebær ... cherry ...
klar suppe med boller broth with meat and
  flour dumplings
kogt(e) boiled
koldt bord cold buffet
kotelet chop
krabbe crab
krabbekløer crab meat *(from the claws)*
kransekage marzipan cake
kringle pastry with almonds, raisins and
  sometimes with cinnamon
krydder savoury, spicy
kræmmerhuse cones with jam and whipped
  cream
kylling chicken
kærnemælkskoldskål cold buttermilk and
  cream soup
kød meat
kødboller meatballs, meat dumplings
kødretter meat dishes
labskovs meat and potato stew
lagkage gâteau
laks salmon
lam lamb
lammekølle leg of lamb
lammeryg saddle of lamb
legeret creamed, thickened
lever liver
leverpostej pâté
lun(t), lune warm
luxusøl extra-strong beer or lager
lys pilsner low-alcohol lager
løg onions
løse ris boiled rice
majskolbe corn on the cob
marineret, marinerede marinated
medisterpølse fried pork sausage
melboller flour dumplings in broth
mineralvand (fruit-flavoured) fizzy drinks
mokka strong after-dinner coffee

morgencomplet breakfast
muslinger mussels
mørbrad fillet
mørbradbøf fried fillet of pork
nougatis ice cream with burnt sugar
nudler noodles
nyrer kidneys
nødder nuts
okse beef
oksehalesuppe oxtail soup
oksetyksteg roast beef
ost(e) ... cheese ...
osteanretning cheese board
pandekager pancakes
pandestegt pan-fried
paneret coated with breadcrumbs
pariserbøf minced beef steak on toast with
  capers, grated horseradish and a raw egg yolk
parisertoast toasted cheese and ham
  sandwich
pattegris sucking pig
peberbøf peppered steak
peberfrugter red or green peppers
peberrod horseradish
perleløg small glazed pearl onions *(fried or
  baked with sugar)*
persille ... parsley ...
pighvar turbot
pillekartofler new potatoes boiled in their
  skins
pilsner lager
platte cold buffet
pocheret, pocherede poached
pommes frites chips, French fries
porrer leeks
purløg chives
pære ... pear ...
pølse(r) sausage(s)
rabarber ... rhubarb ...
rabarbergrød soft rhubarb jelly

ragout stew
rejer prawns, shrimps
rejesalat creamy prawn or shrimp salad
remoulade sweet mustard-and-herb dressing
retter dishes, courses
revelsben spare ribs
ribbenssteg roast spare ribs
ribsgelé redcurrant jelly
ris rice
ris à l'amande cold rice pudding with whipped
  cream, chopped almonds and cherry sauce
ristet, ristede fried, toasted
rogn fish roe
rombudding rum-flavoured blancmange
romfromage rum mousse
rosenkål Brussels sprouts
roulade 1. sponge roll; 2. rolled-up stuffed slice
  of meat; 3. rolled-up joint of meat
rugbrød rye bread
rullepølse sliced streaky pork sausage
rundstykke roll
rødbeder beetroot
rødgrød med fløde soft red-fruit jelly with
  cream
rødkål sweet-and-sour boiled red cabbage
rødspætte plaice
rødvin red wine
røget smoked
røræg scrambled egg
rå raw
rå creme cold vanilla cream sauce
salat 1. plain green tossed salad; 2. vegetables
  or meat or fish in various dressings
selleri celeriac
sennep mustard
sennepsovs mustard sauce
shislik kebab
sild herring
sildesalat marinated herring salad
skaldyr shellfish

skid(d)enæg hardboiled eggs in mustard sauce
skildpaddesuppe turtle soup
skinke ham
skipperlabskovs meat and potato stew
sky meat jelly or juices
smør butter
smørrebrød open sandwiches
snaps clear potato-based liquor
snegle snails
snitte(r) small open sandwich(es)
solbær ... blackcurrant ...
sovs sauce, gravy
spegepølse salami
spegesild marinated herring
spejlæg fried egg
spinat ... spinach ...
sprængt and boiled salt duck
sprængt gås boiled salt goose
sprængt oksebryst boiled brisket of beef
steg roast joint
stegt flæsk med persillesovs fried bacon,
   potatoes served with parsley sauce
stegt(e) fried, roast
stenbider lumpfish
stikkelsbær ... gooseberry ...
stikkelsbærgrød soft gooseberry jelly
stjerneskud open sandwich with a steamed
   and a fried fish fillet and prawns or shrimps
stuvet, stuvede, -stuvning in a creamy
   sauce
sukker sugar
supper soups
surkål sauerkraut *(white cabbage fermented
   with salt)*
surt pickled cucumber, marrow or beetroot
svampe mushrooms
sveske ... prune ...
sveskegrød soft prune jelly
svine ... pork ...
svinekam roast pork

svinemørbrad fillet of pork
svær pork crackling
sylte brawn
syltet, syltede preserved, pickled
syltetøj jam
sød(t), søde sweet
sød-og-sur sweet-and-sour
søtunge sole
tarteletter vol-au-vents
te, the tea
tomat . . . tomato . . .
torsk cod
torskelever cod's liver
torskerogn cod roe
trøfler truffles
tunge 1. tongue; 2. sole
tyttebær cranberries
tærte(r) tart(s)
tør dry
urter herbs
vagtel quail
valnødde . . . walnuts . . .
vanillecreme custard
vanilleis vanilla ice cream
vildt game
vildtsovs redcurrant sauce
vin(e) wine(s)
vinbjergsnegle snails
vindruer grapes
wienerbrød flaky Danish pastry
ymer milk curd, junket *(similar to yoghurt but creamier)*
æble . . . apple . . .
æbleflæsk fried bacon or belly of pork with stewed apples
æblegrød soft apple jelly
æblekage med flødeskum cold apple crumble with whipped cream
æblemost apple juice
æbleskiver small doughnuts

æg egg(s)
æggeblomme egg yolk
æggekage omelette with bacon
ærter peas
øl beer
ørred trout
østers oysters
ål eel

Most Dutch restaurants offer a wide range of dishes in cosy surroundings. Traditional Dutch cooking can still be found in some of the simpler establishments. They may have a sign outside saying **Hollandse Keuken** (Dutch cuisine), or Tourist Information Offices (**VVV**) may be able to tell you where to find them. As in most West European countries, there are also many ethnic restaurants and of these, the Indonesian ones are well worth a visit. Fish, particularly eel and herring in various forms, is very popular, and there are some excellent fish restaurants, especially in fishing towns and villages such as Harderwijk and Volendam.

At lunch-time you may find that a hors d'oeuvre is as much as you can eat. Or you might try some of the filled rolls (**belegde broodjes**) in a cafeteria. If you happen to be in the province of Brabant, a **Brabantse Koffietafel** (cold buffet) may appeal to you. It usually starts with a brandy and a lump of sugar-candy, and is followed by bread, cold meats, cheese (soup is sometimes included) and a pot of coffee.

The Dutch like beer, pils, and, of course, Dutch gin which they drink chilled. **Advocaat**, topped with whipped cream and eaten with a spoon, is also popular. Children like **chocomel** — a cold chocolate drink sold in bottles or cans. Tea is often served with a slice of lemon, so you may have to ask for tea with milk (**thee met melk**).

In most restaurants the staff will be able to speak at least some English. Service charges and VAT (**BTW**) are always included, but some people, mainly tourists, still leave a tip.

....

ORDERING

waiter!
ober!
[ohber]

waitress!
juffrouw *(to young woman)*/mevrouw!
[yuffrow/muhvrow]

can I order please?
kan ik bestellen?
[kan ik bestelluh]

one . . ./two . . .
een . . ./twee . . .
[ayn/tvay]

can I see the menu again?
kan ik de menukaart nog even hebben?
[kan ik deh menewkahrt noch ayvuh hebbuh]

can you bring me another red wine/beer?
nog een glaasje rode wijn/bier alstublieft?
[noch ayn cHlahsyuh rohduh vine/beer alstewbleeft]

could I have the bill please?
ik zou graag afrekenen?
[ik zow cHrahcH afraykenuh]

if the waiter/waitress asks:
   heeft het gesmaakt?
   did you enjoy your meal?

you could reply:
   ja, dank u
   [yah dank oo]
   yes, thank you

SOME BASIC WORDS

beer 'n bier
bottle 'n fles
brandy 'n cognac
bread wat brood *[vat broht]*
coffee koffie
cup 'n kop
dry sec
fork 'n vork
fruit juice 'n vruchtensap *[en vruchtuhsap]*
glass 'n glas *[en chlas]*
gin and tonic 'n gin tonic
half-bottle 'n halve fles *[en halvuh fles]*
hot chocolate 'n warme chocolademelk
  [en varmuh shokolahduhmelk]
ice ijs
knife 'n mes
lager 'n pils
lemonade 'n limonade *[en leemonahduh]*
milk melk
mineral water mineraalwater
  [meenerahlvahter]
mineral water *(fizzy)* mineraalwater met
  prik *[meenerahlvahter met prik]*
napkin 'n servet *[en servet]*
orange juice 'n sinaasappelsap
  [en seenahsappelsap]
pepper peper *[payper]*
red wine rode wijn *[rohduh vine]*
rosé rosé
salt zout *[zowt]*
spoon 'n lepel *[en laypel]*
sugar suiker *[sowker]*
sweet zoet *[zoot]*
tea thee *[tay]*
water water *[vahter]*
whisky 'n whisky
white wine witte wijn *[vittuh vine]*

UNDERSTANDING THE MENU

aan de kassa betalen pay at the cashdesk
aardappelen potatoes
aardappelpuree mashed potatoes
aardbeien strawberries
abrikozencompote stewed apricots
abrikozenvlaai apricot pie
amerikaanse biefstuk ball of minced beef
topped with a fried egg
andijve endive
appelflap apple turnover
appelmoes apple sauce
appelsap applejuice
appeltaart applecake
Ardennerham Ardennes ham
artisjook artichoke
asperges asparagus
augurken gherkins
au jus cooked in gravy
bami goreng Indonesian fried noodle dish with
meat and vegetables
banketletter puff pastry with almond filling
bessenjenever blackcurrant liqueur
biefstuk saignant rare steak
biefstuk van de haas fillet steak
biefstuk van de lende rumpsteak, sirloin
bier van het vat draught beer
bitterballen savoury forcemeat cocktail snacks
bloemkool cauliflower
boerenkool Scotch kale
boerenkool met worst/spek mashed
potatoes with Scotch kale and smoked
sausage/bacon
boerenomelet potato and bacon omelette
bokking (gerookte) (smoked) red herring
bonensla bean salad
**boterham met ... ** ... sandwich
braadworst German sausage
brandewijn brandy

....

brood bread
broodje roll
bruine bonensoep brown bean soup
champignon mushroom
Chateaubriand grilled thick fillet steak
chinese kool Chinese cabbage
chips crisps
chocoladeijs chocolate ice cream
chocoladevla chocolate dessert
chocomel canned or bottled chocolate drink
citroen lemon
citroenthee lemon tea
citroenvla lemon custard or mousse
dagmenu/dagschotel menu/dish of the day
dame blanche ice cream with chocolate sauce
donker bier dark beer
doperwten garden peas
drie in de pan small pancakes with currants
    and raisins
druiven blauwe/witte black/white grapes
duitse biefstuk beef and onion hamburgers
eieren eggs
eisbein pickled upper leg of pork
erwtensoep pea soup
fazant pheasant
filet american hamburger
filosoof shepherd's pie
flensjes thin pancakes
forel trout
frambozen raspberries
frikandel sausage
ganzeleverpastei goose liver pâté
garnalencocktail prawn cocktail
garnalensaus shrimp sauce
gebakjes small cakes
gebakken fried
gebakken bloedworst fried black pudding
gebakken ei met spek fried egg with bacon
gebakken forel met amandelen fried trout
    with almonds

gebraden eend met sinaasappel roast duck
à l'orange
gebraden fazant roast pheasant
gebraden gehakt roast meatloaf
gebraden haantje fried chicken
gehakt minced beef
gehaktbal minced beef and pork rissole
gekookte achterham boiled gammon
gekookte mosselen boiled mussels
gemarineerd rundvlees marinated beef
gepocheerde zalm met Hollandse saus
poached salmon with Hollandaise sauce
gerookte smoked
geroosterd brood toast
gestoofde paling stewed eel
gevulde koek pasty with almond filling
gevulde omelet met groene kruiden
omelette with green herbs
gevulde stuffed
goelasjsoep goulash soup
groene haring first-of-the-season lightly
salted herring
groenten vegetables
groentesoep vegetable soup
haas hare
hachée diced stewing steak
hardgekookt ei hard-boiled egg
haring herring
hazepastei hare pâté
hazepeper jugged hare
heilbot halibut
hollandse biefstuk thick slice of frying steak
hom soft roe
honingkoek type of gingerbread
hutspot (met klapstuk) mashed potatoes
with carrots, onions, breast or rib of beef
huzarensla potato salad with beetroot,
gherkin, salmon, sardines etc
ijs ice cream
jachtschotel shepherd's pie

jenever Dutch gin
jonge klare young Dutch gin
kaas cheese
kaassoesje cheese puff
kabeljauw cod
kadetje soft roll
kalfs-fricassee veal fricassee in thick white
  sauce
kalfsniertjes calf's kidneys
kalfsoester escalope of veal
kalfsschnitzel veal schnitzel
kalkoen turkey
kapucijners marrowfat peas
karbonade chops
kerriesoep curry soup
kersen cherries
kersenvlaai cherry pie
kervel chervil
kinderijsje small ice cream
kinderportie child's portion
kindersurprise children's ice cream
kip chicken
kip aan 't spit spit-roasted chicken
knoflook garlic
koffie coffee
koffietafel set cold buffet lunch
kogelbiefstuk thick end of rump
komkommer cucumber
koninginnesoep cream of chicken soup
kool cabbage
korenwijn mature malted Dutch gin
koude gerechten/schotels cold dishes
kreeft lobster
kroepoek prawn crackers
kuikenbouten chicken legs
kuit hard roe
kwark soft white cheese
kwarktaart cheesecake
lamsbout leg of lamb
lams coteletjes lamb cutlets

lamsragout lamb stew
lamstong lamb's tongue
landwijn table wine
lekkerbekjes whiting fillets fried in batter
leverworst liver sausage
licht bier light beer
limburgse vlaai fruit flan
linzen lentils
loempia Indonesian spring roll
maaltijdsoep thick soup
maiskolf corn on the cob
maiskorrels sweetcorn
makreel mackerel
menu van de dag today's menu
mihoen goreng fried rice with vegetables and
  meat
mosselen mussels
mosselen in het zuur pickled mussels
nagerecht dessert
nasi goreng Indonesian fried rice dish with
  meat and vegetables
nieuwe haring salted herring
oesters oysters
olijven groene/zwarte green/black olives
omelet met ham ham omelette
omelet met kaas cheese omelette
ontbijtkoek type of gingerbread
ontbijtspek bacon
op zij as a side dish
ossestaartsoep oxtail soup
ossetong ox tongue
oude klare mature Dutch gin
paling eel
paling in gelei jellied eel
paling in het groen eel in sorrel sauce and
  green herbs
pannekoek met stroop/suiker pancake with
  syrup/sugar
pasteitje small vol-au-vent
patates frites chips

patrijs partridge
perencompote stewed pears
perziken peaches
peterselie parsley
picallily pickles
poffertjes tiny pancakes dusted with icing
    sugar and eaten with butter
pommes frites French fries
pompelmoes grapefruit
prei leek
preisoep leek soup
reebout haunch of venison
reerug saddle of venison
regenboogforel rainbow trout
rijst rice
rivierkreeft crayfish
rode bieten beetroot
rode kool red cabbage
rode wijn red wine
roerei scrambled eggs
roggebrood rye bread
rolmops rollmops, pickled herring
rookvlees smoked beef or horse sliced very
    thin *(eaten on bread)*
rookworst smoked sausage
roomijs ice cream
roomijstaart ice cream gâteau
roomsoes éclair
rosbief roast beef
rundvlees beef
sate Indonesian kebab
saucijzenbroodje sausage roll
saus sauce
schapevlees mutton
schartong lemon sole
schelvis haddock
schelvislever haddock liver
schildpadsoep turtle soup
schnitzel veal cutlet
schol plaice

schorseneren salsify
schuimomelet sweet omelette
schuimpje meringue
sinaasappelsap orange juice
sjis kebab shish kebab
slaatje salad
slagroom whipped cream
slagroom taart whipped cream cake
slagroomwafels waffles with whipped cream
soep Lady Curzon turtle soup finished with cream and a pinch of curry powder
soep van de dag soup of the day
spaanse omelet omelette with vegetables
spek bacon
spekpannekoek pancake with bacon
sperziebonen French beans
spiegelei fried egg
spijskaart menu
spinazie spinach
spruiten/spruitjes Brussels sprouts
taart cake
tarbot turbot
tartaar raw minced steak with a raw egg *(steak tartare)*
thee met citroen/melk en suiker tea with lemon/milk and sugar
tomatensoep (met gehaktballetjes) tomato soup (with small meat balls)
tompoes vanilla slice
tong met champignons sole with mushrooms
tongrolletjes rolled fillets of sole
tosti toasted sandwich
tuinbonen broad beans
uiensoep onion soup
uitsmijter slice of bread topped with slice of ham and fried egg
uitsmijter met kaas slice of bread topped with slice of cheese and fried egg
varkensbiefstuk pork fillet

varkensfricandeau pork fricandeau
  (larded and braised pork)
varkenshaas pork fillet
varkensoester pork escalope
vermicellisoep chicken noodle soup
verse haring fresh herring
verse oesters fresh oysters
vis fish
volkorenbrood wholemeal bread
voorgerecht starter, hors d'oeuvre
warme gerechten/schotels hot dishes
wijnkaart winelist
wijting whiting
wild game
witte bonen dried white beans
witte wijn white wine
worstebroodje sausage roll
worteltjes carrots
zachtgekookt eitje soft-boiled egg
zalm salmon
zalmslaatje salmon salad
zeepaling sea-eel
zeetong sole
zigeunerschnitzel schnitzel with garlic and
  paprika
zoute haring salted herring
zure haring pickled herring
zuurkool met spek sauerkraut with bacon
zwezerik sweetbread

MEAL-TIMES in Finland are generally early: breakfast (**aamiainen**) is from 7 to 10 a.m., lunch (**lounas**) from 11 a.m. to 2 p.m., dinner (**päivällinen**) from 4 to 7 p.m., and supper (**illallinen**) from 7 p.m. to midnight. Meals are also served outside these times.

Restaurants (**ravintola**) serve international and Finnish cuisine, and if you are in Helsinki, it is certainly worth your while to try one of the many Russian restaurants. Italian, Spanish, Greek, Chinese and French food is also available, as is vegetarian food (**kasvisruoka**). A service charge of 15% is always included, but tips are not refused. For ordinary everyday dishes (**kotiruoka**) you could try one of the many **kahvila/baari** (café/bar) where you will always find the traditional Finnish favourites **kaalikääryleet** (stuffed cabbage leaves) and **lihapullat** (meat balls).

Alcohol regulations in Finland are very strict (sale of alcohol is a state monopoly) and although beer is available from 9 a.m. onwards, spirits are not served before 11 a.m. Restaurants are coded according to the type of licence: 'A' means fully licensed, 'B' means licensed for wine and beer only, and no coding means that alcohol is not available.

ORDERING

excuse me, waiter!
anteeksi, tarjoilija!
[un-tex-see tar-yoy-lee-ya]

excuse me, miss!
anteeksi, neiti!
[un-tex-see nay-tee]

37

can I order, please?
haluaisin tilata
[ha-loo-ı-sin tee-lah-ta]

one . . ./two . . .
yksi . . ./kaksi . . .
[ewk-si/kak-si]

that's for me/him
se on minulle/hänelle
[seh on mee-nool-leh/ha-nel-leh]

can I see the menu again?
saanko nähdä ruokalistan uudestaan?
[sahn-koh na-da rwor-ka-lis-tan oo-des-tahn]

can you bring me another red wine/beer?
voitteko tuoda minulle lisää punaviiniä/olutta?
[voyt-teh-koh twor-dah mee-nool-leh lees-air poo-na-veen-ee-a/oloo-ta]

could I have the bill, please?
saanko laskun?
[sahn-koh las-koon]

if the waiter/waitress says:
  toivottavasti piditte ateriasta
  [toyvot-tavastee peedeet-teh atehree-asta]
  I hope you enjoyed your meal

you could say:
  kiitos — ruoka oli oikein maukasta
  [kee-tos rwor-ka ol-ee oy-kayn mao-kas-ta]
  yes, thank you — it was very nice

SOME BASIC WORDS

beer olut *[ol-oot]*
bottle pullo *[pool-loh]*
brandy konjakki *[kon-yak-kee]*
bread leipä *[lay-pa]*

coffee kahvi *[kah-vee]*
cup kuppi *[koop-pee]*
dry kuiva *[koo-ee-va]*
fork haarukka *[hah-rook-ka]*
fruit juice hedelmämehu *[heh-del-ma-may-hoo]*
glass lasi *[lah-see]*
gin and tonic gin ja tonic *[gin ya tonik]*
half-bottle puoli pulloa *[pwor-lee pool-loh-ah]*
hot chocolate kaakao *[kah-kao]*
ice jää *[yair]*
knife veitsi *[vayt-see]*
lager kalja *[kal-ya]*
lemonade limonaadi *[lee-mo-naah-dee]*
milk maito *[mi-tor]*
mineral water mineraalivesi *[mee-ner-aah-lee-ves-see]*
mineral water *(fizzy)* hiilihapollinen mineraalivesi *[hee-lee-ha-pol-lee-nen mee-ner-aah-lee-ves-see]*
napkin lautasliina *[laot-us-lee-na]*
orange juice appelsiinimehu *[ahp-pel-see-nee-may-hoo]*
pepper pippuri *[pip-poor-ree]*
red wine punaviini *[poo-na-vee-nee]*
rosé rosé *[ros-ay]*
salt suola *[swor-la]*
spoon lusikka *[loo-sik-ka]*
sugar sokeri *[sock-ay-ree]*
sweet makea *[mak-ay-a]*
tea tee *[tay]*
water vesi *[ves-see]*
whisky viski *[vis-kee]*
white wine valkoviini *[vahl-ko-vee-nee]*

UNDERSTANDING THE MENU

aamiainen/aamupala breakfast
ahven perch

alkoholijuoma alcoholic drink
alkupalat starter, hors d'oeuvre
ananas pineapple
ankerias eel
ankka duck
appelsiini orange
appelsiinimarmelaadi marmalade
appelsiinimehu orange juice
aprikoosikiisseli apricot dessert
aromivoi herb butter
banaani banana
blinit Russian buckwheat pancakes
elävä ravinto 'living food' *(vegetarian dishes
  that consist of germinated wheat, bean sprouts,
  raw fruit and vegetables)*
eturuoka warm starter
forelli trout
graavi lohi salmon cured with salt, pepper,
  sugar and dill
greippi grapefruit
grillipihvi grilled steak
hampurilainen hamburger
hanhenpaisti roast goose
hapankaali sauerkraut
hapanleipä sour black rye bread
hauki pike
hedelmämehu fruit juice
hedelmäsalaatti fruit salad
herkkusienikeitto mushroom soup
herneet peas
hernekeitto pea soup with pork
hiiligrillattu pihvi charcoal steak
hillo jam
hyydytetty muna poached egg
hyytelö jelly
häränkyljys porterhouse steak
häränleike Chateaubriand, beef cutlet
häränseläke fillet of beef
Janssonin kiusaus sliced potatoes baked with
  anchovies in cream sauce

jauheliha minced meat
jauhelihakastike minced meat gravy
jauhelihapihvit hamburger steaks
juusto cheese
juustokohokas cheese soufflé
juustopasteija cheese pasty
juustosalaatti cheese salad
juustotarjotin cheese board
juustovoileipä cheese sandwich
jänispaisti roast hare
jäätelö ice cream
jäävesi iced water
kaakao hot chocolate
kaalikääryleet cabbage leaves stuffed with
  rice or minced beef
kaalipiirakka cabbage pasty
kahvi coffee
kahviaamiainen continental breakfast
kakku cake
kala fish
kala-vihanneskeitto fish and vegetable soup
kalakukko regional pasty, made of fish and
  pork in rye pastry
kalapihvi fish cake
kalapuikko fish finger
kalapyörykkä fish cake
kalja very light beer
kalkkuna turkey
kampela flatfish, flounder
kana chicken
kanakeitto chicken soup
kananmuna egg
kananrinta breast of chicken
karjalanpaisti Karelian stew of beef, pork and
  lamb
karjalanpiirakka rice pie in thin rye pastry
karpalo cranberry
karviainen/karviaismarja gooseberry
kasvislounas vegetarian lunch
kasvisruoka vegetarian food

....

katkarapu/katkaravut shrimps
kaurapuuro porridge
kaviaari caviar
keitetty kananmuna boiled egg
keitetyt kuoriperunat potatoes boiled in
their jackets
keitto soup
kerma cream
kermakakku cream cake
keskiolut medium strong beer
kesäkeitto mixed vegetable soup made with
milk
ketsuppi ketchup
kiisseli sweet berry or fruit dessert, thickened
with potato or cornflour
kinkku ham
kinkkumunakas ham omelette
kinkkuvoileipä ham sandwich
kirjolohi rainbow trout
kirkas lihaliemi consommé
kivennäisvesi mineral water
kokojyväleipä wholemeal bread
kolja haddock
koskenkorva Finnish vodka
kotitekoinen home-made
kovaksi keitetty kananmuna hard-boiled
egg
kuha pike-perch
kukkakaali cauliflower
Kuningas Oskarin leike King Oskar's cutlet
(veal)
kurkku cucumber
kääretorttu Swiss roll
laivurinpihvit skipper's steak *(stewed steak)*
laktovegetariaaninen lacto-vegetarian
lammas lamb
lampaankyljys lamb chops or cutlets
lampaanpaisti roast lamb
lanttulaatikko baked swede purée, flavoured
with syrup

lasimestarin silli pickled herring
leipä bread
leipävanukas bread pudding
leivos pastry
liha meat
lihakeitto beef and vegetable soup
lihakääryle meat roll
lihaliemi beef stock
lihamureke meat loaf
lihapasteija meat pasty
lihapiirakka meat pie
lihapullat meat balls
lihapyörkkä meat ball
liharuoka meat dish
likööri liqueur
Lindströmin pihvit beefburgers containing
  potato and beetroot
linssileikkeet lentil burgers
lohi salmon
lohikeitto salmon and potato soup
lohivoileipä salmon sandwich
lämmin voileipä fried sandwich
maito milk
majoneesikastike mayonnaise dressing
makkara sausage
maksa liver
maksalaatikko liver and rice stew flavoured
  with syrup
mannaryynivanukas semolina pudding
mansikka strawberry
mansikkajäätelö strawberry ice cream
mansikkakiisseli strawberry dessert,
  thickened with potato flour
marenki meringue
marmelaati jam
makea sweet
mehu juice
meloni melon
merenherkut seafood
meriantura sole

metso woodgrouse
mineraalivesi mineral water
mokkajäätelö coffee flavoured ice-cream
muna egg
munakas omelette
munakastike white sauce with finely chopped
  egg
munakokkeli scrambled eggs
munariisipasteija egg and rice pasty
munavoileipä egg sandwich
munia ja pekonia bacon and eggs
munkit doughnuts
mustikkakiisseli bilberry dessert, thickened
  with potato flour
mäti roe
nakki frankfurter
nakkisämpylä frankfurter in a long bread roll
naudanliha beef
näkkileipä crispbread
ohukaiset pancakes
olut beer
omena apple
omenamehu apple juice
osterit oysters
paahtoleipä toast
paahtopaisti roast beef
paahtovanukas caramel custard
paistettu fried, roast
paistettu ankka roast duck
paistettu kalkkuna roast turkey
paistettu kana roast chicken
paistettu kinkku roast ham
paistettu metso roast woodgrouse
paistettu muna fried egg
paistetut perunat fried potatoes
pannukakku large pancake baked in oven
paprika red pepper
pavut beans
parsa asparagus
parsakaali broccoli

parsakeitto asparagus soup
pasteija pasty
patonki French stick
pehmeäksi keitetty kananmuna soft-boiled
  egg
pekoni bacon
peltopyy partridge
persikka peach
peruna potato
perunasalaatti potato salad
perunasose mashed potatoes
pihvi steak
piimä sour milk, buttermilk
pinaatti spinach
pippuripihvi pepper steak
porkkana carrot
poro reindeer
porsaan pork
porsaan paisti roast pork
porsaankyljys pork chop
porsas pork
portviini port
punajuuri beetroot
punaviini red wine
puolukkapuuro lingonberry *(type of
  cranberry)* dessert made with semolina
purjo leek
purolohi trout
pyttipannu potato and meat hash
pähkinäleikkeet nut burgers
päivän kotiruoka daily special
päivän lounas luncheon special
pääruoka main course
päärynä pear
raastevati grated mixed root vegetables
rahkapiirakka type of cheesecake with raisins
ranskalainen munakas French omelette
ranskalainen salaatti mixed vegetable salad
  in mayonnaise
ranskalainen salaattikastike French dressing

ranskalaiset perunat chips, French fries
ranskanleipä French bread
rapu/ravut crayfish
riisi rice
riisivanukas rice pudding
rommi rum
ruisleipä black rye bread
salaatti salad
savusilli kipper
sianliha pork
sienet mushrooms
sienikastike wild mushroom sauce
sienikeitto mushroom soup *(made with Finnish wild mushrooms)*
sienisalaatti mushroom salad
silakka Baltic herring
silakkapihvit fried Baltic herrings
silli herring
sillisalaatti (rosolli) mixed vegetable salad with pickled herring
sima mead *(home-made lemonade-type drink)*
sinappi mustard
sipuli onion
sipulipihvit steaklets with onion
sitruuna lemon
soijapyörykät soya burgers
sorsa wild duck
stroganoff beef stroganoff
suklaakakku chocolate cake
suklaakastike chocolate sauce
suklaakiisseli chocolate dessert
suklaakohokas chocolate soufflé
sämpylä roll
talon/tapaan chef's special
tilliliha boiled veal or lamb in dill sauce
tilliperunat potatoes boiled with dill
tippaleipä May-day fritter *(deep-fried thin strands of doughnut-type mixture)*
tomaatti tomato
tomaattikastike tomato sauce

tomaattikeitto tomato soup
tomaatimehu tomato juice
tonnikala tuna fish
turska cod
täytekakku gâteau
uudet perunat new potatoes
vaalea olut lager
vadelma/vattu raspberry
valkoviini white wine
vaniljajäätelö chocolate ice cream
vaniljakastike custard
vasikankotletti veal cutlet
vasikka veal
verivanukas black pudding
vesimeloni watermelon
vihanneskeitto vegetable soup
vihannesvati vegetable platter
vihersalaatti green salad
vihreä pippuri green pepper
vihreät pavut French beans
viili Finnish-style yoghurt
viineri Danish pastry
viinilista wine list
viinirypäleet grapes
virvoitusjuomat beverages, soft drinks
voileipä sandwich
voileipäpöytä Finnish cold buffet
  (smörgåsbord)
väkijuoma spirits
wieninleike breaded veal escalope
wieninleipä Danish pastry

WHEREVER you are in France and whatever your budget, the food will always be of excellent quality. Each region has its own specialities based on local produce which guarantee good value for money. You can choose from three types of restaurant: the **routier**, an inexpensive roadside restaurant; the **brasserie**, which serves the French version of fast food and where the food is less sophisticated than the traditional **restaurant**.

Some regions are well known not only for their cuisine but also for their wine. Bourgogne is famous for its red wine sauces and its snails in garlic butter, and it produces some of the finest wines in France. In the south-west, you should sample the beautiful clarets of the Bordeaux region and the unique grape brandy from the town of Cognac. Normandy is renowned for its dairy produce, in particular for **camembert** cheese, and also for ciders and the strong apple brandy, **calvados**. Provence produces a lovely fruity rosé wine which provides the perfect accompaniment to the regional speciality **bouillabaisse** (spicy fish soup), which should not be missed. In the north-east of France, you can celebrate in style in the town of Reims with a glass of **champagne**.

A wide range of ethnic food is also available, for example, North African, African, Creole, Vietnamese, Brazilian, Russian and many more.

Menus and prices are always on display outside so don't hesitate to shop around before choosing a restaurant: most French people do! Children are always welcome and often a children's menu is available. A 15% service charge is always included in the prices shown on the menu but it is the custom to leave a tip for the waiter or waitress.

ORDERING

excuse me!
s'il vous plaît!
[seelvooplay]

can I order please?
je peux commander s'il vous plaît?
[jer per kohmon-day seelvooplay]

one . . ./two . . .
un (une) . . ./deux . . .
[an (oon)/der]

that's for me/him
c'est pour moi/lui
[say por mwah/lwee]

can I see the menu again?
est-ce que je peux revoir la carte, s'il vous plaît?
[esker jer per rervwahr lah kart seelvooplay]

can you bring me another red wine/beer?
j'aimerais un autre verre de vin rouge/une autre bière
[jaym-ray an-ohtr vair der van rooj/oon-ohtr bee-yair]

could I have the bill please?
l'addition, s'il vous plaît
[ladees-yon seelvooplay]

if the waiter/waitress asks you:
  vous avez bien mangé?
  [vooz-ah-vay bee-yan monjay]
  did you enjoy your meal?

you can say, trying your hardest to pronounce
the French nasal 'N' in an authentic manner:
  oui, c'était très bon
  [wee saytay tray bon]
  yes, it was delicious

....

SOME BASIC WORDS

beer une bière *[oon bee-yair]*
bottle une bouteille *[oon boo-tay]*
brandy un cognac *[aN kohn-yak]*
bread du pain *[dew paN]*
coffee un café *[aN kah-fay]*
cup une tasse *[oon tahs]*
dry sec
fork une fourchette *[oon foor-shet]*
fruit juice un jus de fruits *[aN joo der frwee]*
glass un verre *[aN vair]*
gin and tonic un gin-tonic
half-bottle une demi-bouteille *[oon der-mee boo-tay]*
hot chocolate un chocolat chaud *[aN shokoh-lah shoh]*
ice des glaçons *[day glahsoN]*
knife un couteau *[aN koo-toh]*
lager un demi *[aN der-mee]*
lemonade une limonade *[oon leemohnad]*
milk du lait *[dew lay]*
mineral water de l'eau minérale *[der loh meenay-rahl]*
mineral water *(fizzy)* de l'eau minérale (gazeuse) *[der loh meenay-rahl gazerz]*
napkin une serviette *[oon sairv-yet]*
orange juice un jus d'orange *[aN joo dohroNj]*
pepper du poivre *[dew pwahvr]*
red wine du vin rouge *[dew vaN rooj]*
rosé du vin rosé *[dew vaN rohzay]*
salt du sel
spoon une cuiller *[oon kwee-yair]*
sugar du sucre *[dew sookr]*
sweet doux *[doo]*
tea un thé *[aN tay]*
water de l'eau *[der loh]*
whisky un whisky
white wine du vin blanc *[dew vaN bloN]*

UNDERSTANDING THE MENU

à emporter to take away
à l'ail with garlic
à la normande in cream sauce
à la provençale cooked in olive oil with
  tomatoes, garlic and herbs
agneau lamb
ail garlic
amande almond
ananas pineapple
anchois anchovies
andouillette small spicy tripe sausage
anguille eel
appellation d'origine contrôlée guarantee of
  the quality of wine
artichaut artichoke
asperge asparagus
assiette anglaise selection of cold meats
au choix . . . choice of . . .
aux câpres in caper sauce
avocat avocado
bavette à l'échalote grilled beef with shallots
béarnaise with bearnaise sauce
beurre butter
beurre noir dark melted butter
bière (blonde) lager
bière brune bitter; dark beer
bifteck steak
bisque de homard lobster bisque
blanc white
blanc de blancs white wine from white grapes
blanquette de veau veal stew
boeuf beef
boeuf bourguignon beef cooked in red wine
boeuf en daube beef casserole
boeuf mode beef stew with carrots
boissons pilotes most common drinks *(low-
  priced)*
bouchée à la reine vol au vent

....

boudin black pudding
bouillabaisse spicy fish soup from the Midi
bouillon de légumes vegetable broth
boulette meatball
braisé braised
brandade de morue cod in cream and garlic
brochet pike
brochette kebab
cabillaud cod
café black coffee
café au lait white coffee
café crème white coffee
café liégeois iced coffee with cream
caille quail
calmar squid
calvados apple brandy from Normandy
canard duck
canard à l'orange duck in orange sauce
canard laqué Peking duck
caneton duckling
carbonnade beef casseroled in beer
carte menu
cassoulet pork, sausage and bean casserole
céleri rémoulade celeriac in mustard dressing
cêpes ceps *(mushroom)*
cerises cherries
cervelas saveloy *(highly seasoned sausage made from brains)*
cervelle brains
champignons mushrooms
champignons de Paris button mushrooms *(cultivated)*
chanterelles chanterelles *(mushroom)*
chantilly whipped cream
chèvre goat's milk cheese
chevreuil venison
chocolat chaud hot chocolate
chou cabbage
choux de Bruxelles Brussels sprouts
chou-fleur cauliflower

choucroute sauerkraut *(pickled shredded cabbage cooked with bacon and sausages)*
cidre bouché dry cider
cidre doux sweet cider
citron lemon
citron pressé fresh lemon juice
civet de lièvre jugged hare
colin hake
concombre cucumber
confit d'oie goose preserve
coq au vin chicken in red wine
coque cockle
coquilles Saint-Jacques scallops
côtelette chop
côtelette de porc pork chop
coulis sweet or savoury creamy sauce
coupe ice cream dessert
couscous steamed semolina with a spicy meat and vegetable stew
crabe crab
crème cream, creamy sauce or dessert
crème anglaise custard
crème d'asperges cream of asparagus soup
crème de bolets cream of mushroom soup
crème pâtissière fine custard
crêpe pancake
crêpes Suzette flambéed pancakes with orange sauce
cresson watercress
crevette grise shrimp
crevette rose prawn
croque-Madame toasted cheese sandwich with ham and a fried egg
croque-Monsieur toasted cheese sandwich with ham
crudités selection of salads, chopped raw vegetables
crustacés shellfish
cuisses de grenouille frog's legs
cuissot de chevreuil haunch of venison

déjeuner lunch
demi 1. small draught beer; 2. half litre of wine
demi-sec medium dry
diabolo menthe mint cordial with lemonade
digestif liqueur
dinde turkey
dîner dinner
doux sweet
eau minérale mineral water
eau minérale gazeuse sparkling mineral
   water
échalote shallot
écrevisse freshwater crayfish
endive chicory
en gelée in aspic
entrecôte rib steak
entrecôte maître d'hôtel steak with butter
   and parsley
entrée starter
entremets puddings
épinards à la crème spinach with cream
escalope à la crème escalope in cream sauce
escalope panée slice of veal in breadcrumbs
escargot snail
esquimau ice cream on a stick
faisan pheasant
farci stuffed
filet fillet
filet de boeuf Rossini fillet of beef with foie
   gras
financière rich sauce *(served with sweetbread,
   dumplings etc)*
flageolets kidney beans
flan egg custard
foie de veau veal liver
foie gras fine goose or duck liver pâté
foies de volaille chicken livers
fondue Swiss dish of cheese melted in white
   wine
fondue bourguignonne meat fondue

fraises strawberries
framboises raspberries
frisée aux lardons curly endive with bacon
frit deep-fried
frites chips, French fries
fromage cheese
fruits de mer seafood
galantine cold meat in aspic
galette round flat cake; wholemeal pancake
garni with chips or rice and vegetables
gâteau cake
gibelotte de lapin rabbit stewed in white wine
gibier game
gigot d'agneau roast leg of lamb
glace ice cream
grand veneur sauce for game
gratin baked cheese dish
gratin dauphinois thinly-sliced potatoes
    baked with cream and grated cheese
gratinée baked onion soup
grillade grilled meat
hachis Parmentier shepherd's pie
hareng mariné marinated herring
haricot de mouton mutton stew with haricot
    beans
haricots blancs haricot beans
haricots verts green beans
homard lobster
homard à l'américaine lobster in white wine
    and tomato sauce
hors-d'oeuvre starter
huîtres oysters
îles flottantes floating islands *(poached
    whisked egg whites on top of custard)*
jambon ham
julienne soup with chopped vegetables
jus d'orange orange juice
kir white wine with blackcurrant liqueur
lait milk
laitue lettuce

langouste crayfish
langoustine scampi
langue de boeuf ox tongue
lapin rabbit
lapin chasseur rabbit in white wine and herbs
légume vegetable
lentille lentil
lièvre hare
limande dab, lemon sole
lotte burbot *(fish)*
loup au fenouil bass with fennel
macédoine de légumes mixed vegetables
magret de canard duck breast
maquereau au vin blanc mackerel in white
 wine sauce
marc grape brandy
marrons chestnuts
menu gastronomique gourmet menu
menu touristique economy menu
millefeuille custard slice
morilles morels *(mushroom)*
morue cod
moules marinière mussels in white wine
mousse de foie light liver pâté
moutarde mustard
mouton mutton
muscat sweet white wine
nature plain
navarin mutton stew with vegetables
navet turnip
noisette hazelnut
noix walnut
oeuf à la coque boiled egg
oeuf dur hard boiled egg
oeuf en gelée egg in aspic
oeuf mayonnaise egg mayonnaise
oeuf poché poached egg
oeufs brouillés scrambled eggs
oeufs en meurette poached eggs in wine sauce
oeuf sur le plat fried egg

oie goose
oignon onion
omelette aux fines herbes omelette with herbs
omelette nature plain omelette
orange givrée orange sorbet served in the orange
oseille sorrel
pain bread
palourde clam
pamplemousse grapefruit
panaché shandy
pané breaded
pâtes pasta
paupiettes de veau veal olives
pêche peach
perdrix partridge
petits pois peas
petite friture whitebait
pied de porc pig's trotters
pintade guinea fowl
pipérade basque egg dish with tomatoes
pissaladière provençal dish similar to pizza
plat du jour today's set menu
plateau de fromages cheese board
plateau de fruits de mer seafood platter
poire pear
poireau leek
poire belle-Hélène pear in chocolate sauce
poisson fish
poivre pepper *(seasoning)*
poivron green or red pepper
pomme apple
pomme de terre potato
pommes dauphine potato croquettes
pommes de terre à l'anglaise steamed potatoes
pommes de terre sautées fried potatoes
pommes frites chips, French fries
pommes vapeur boiled potatoes

....

porc pork
pot au feu beef and vegetable stew
potage soup
potée vegetable and meat stew
poularde fattened chicken
poule au pot chicken and vegetable stew
poule au riz chicken and rice
poulet basquaise chicken with ham, tomatoes
    and peppers
poulet rôti roast chicken
poutargue smoked fish roe
pression draught beer
prune plum
pruneau prune
purée (de pommes de terre) mashed
    potatoes
quenelle meat or fish dumpling
quiche lorraine egg and bacon quiche
râble de lièvre saddle of hare
raie au beurre noir skate in black butter
raisin grapes
ratatouille stew of courgettes, peppers,
    aubergines and tomatoes
rillettes potted pork and goose meat
ris de veau veal sweetbread
riz rice
rognon kidney
rosé rosé wine
rôti 1. joint; 2. roast
rouge red
rouget mullet
salade lettuce with oil and vinegar dressing
salade niçoise salad with olives, tomatoes,
    anchovies, green beans and peppers
salade russe diced vegetables in mayonnaise
salmis game stew
sanglier wild boar
sauce béarnaise sauce made from egg yolks,
    lemon juice or vinegar, butter and herbs
sauce béchamel white sauce

sauce hollandaise rich sauce served with fish
sauce matelote wine sauce
sauce mornay white sauce with cheese
sauce ravigote dressing with shallots and
  herbs
saucisse sausage
saucisson salami-type sausage
saumon salmon
saumon fumé smoked salmon
sec dry
sel salt
selon arrivage depending on availability
service compris service included
service 15% inclus 15% service charge
  included
soufflé au fromage cheese soufflé
soufflé au Grand Marnier soufflé with
  orange liqueur
soup thick soup
soupe à l'oignon onion soup
soupe au pistou thick vegetable soup with
  basil
soupe de légumes vegetable soup
soupe de poissons fish soup
steak au poivre pepper steak
steak frites steak and chips
steak haché minced beef
steak tartare raw minced beef with a raw egg
tajine North African stew of lamb, vegetables
  and prunes cooked in an earthenware dish
tarte aux myrtilles bilberry tart
tarte aux pommes apple tart or pie
tartelette small tart or pie
tarte tatin baked apple dish
tartine buttered slice of bread
terrine pâté
terrine du chef chef's pâté
thé tea
thé à la menthe mint tea
thé au lait tea with milk

thé citron lemon tea
thon tuna fish
tilleul lime tea
tomates farcies stuffed tomatoes
tournedos fillet steak
tripes à la mode de Caen tripe in spicy
  tomato sauce
truite au bleu poached trout
truite aux amandes trout with almonds
truite meunière fried trout
veau veal
velouté d'asperges cream of asparagus soup
velouté de tomates cream of tomato soup
verveine verbena tea
viande meat
vichyssoise cold vegetable soup
vinaigrette oil and vinegar dressing
volaille poultry
yaourt yogurt

MOST restaurants will have a large variety of dishes available and you can usually expect generous portions of good quality food. In particular, there will be an especially wide choice of vegetables and salads. All restaurants are licensed, with a large selection of drinks, especially wines.

Menus may look quite different depending on whether you are in the north or in the south, and it is worthwhile sampling local specialities. Many places will display a separate **Tageskarte** (menu of the day) in addition to their normal menu.

Due to the influx of foreign labour over the past decades there are a large number of ethnic restaurants, mainly Italian, Spanish, Greek, Turkish and Yugoslavian. You will also find French and Chinese restaurants, but very few Indian ones.

For your dessert, be sure to sample some of the cakes and gâteaux which are generally of the finest quality.

Your bill will normally include service and VAT (**MwSt**), but it is customary to tip the waiter when paying your bill or to leave some small change on the table.

ORDERING

excuse me . . .
Verzeihung . . .
[fairtsioong . . .]

can I order please?
ich möchte gern bestellen
[ish murshtuh gairn beshtellen]

....

one . . ./two . . .
einmal . . ./zweimal . . .
[ın-mal/tsvı-mal]

that's for me/him
das ist für mich/ihn
[dass ist fewr mish/een]

can I see the menu again?
kann ich die Speisekarte nochmal sehen?
[kann ish dee shpızuh-kartuh nokmal zay-en]

can you bring me another red wine/beer?
können Sie mir noch einen Rotwein/ein Bier
bringen?
[kurnen zee meer nok ın-en roht-vın/ın beer bring-en]

could I have the bill please?
ich hätte gern die Rechnung
[ish hettuh gairn dee reshnoong]

if the waiter/waitress says:
  hat's geschmeckt?
  [hats guhshmeckt]
  did you enjoy your meal?

you could reply:
  ja, danke
  [yah dankuh]
  yes, thank you

SOME BASIC WORDS

beer ein Bier *[beer]*
bottle eine Flasche *[flashuh]*
brandy ein Weinbrand *[vınbrant]*
bread Brot *[broht]*
coffee ein Kaffee *[kaffay]*
cup eine Tasse *[tassuh]*
dry trocken

fork eine Gabel *[gahbel]*
fruit juice ein Fruchtsaft *[frooktzaft]*
glass ein Glas *[glahss]*
gin and gonic ein Gin Tonic
half-bottle eine halbe Flasche *[halbuh flashuh]*
hot chocolate eine heiße Schokolade *[hissuh shockohlahduh]*
ice Eis *[iss]*
knife ein Messer
lager ein helles Bier *[helluh-ss beer]*
lemonade eine Limonade *[limonahde]*
milk Milch *[milsh]*
mineral water *(still)* ein Tafelwasser *[tahfelvasser]*
mineral water *(fizzy)* ein Mineralwasser *[minerahlvasser]*
napkin eine Serviette *[zairvee-ettuh]*
orange juice ein Orangensaft *[oronjenzaft]*
pepper Pfeffer
red wine ein Rotwein *[rohtvin]*
rosé ein Rosé *[rohzay]*
salt Salz *[zalts]*
spoon ein Löffel *[lurfel]*
sugar Zucker *[tsoocker]*
sweet süß *[sewss]*
tea ein Tee *[tay]*
water Wasser *[vasser]*
whisky ein Whisky
white wine ein Weißwein *[viss-vin]*

UNDERSTANDING THE MENU

Am Spieß roast on a spit
Apfel im Schlafrock baked apples in puff pastry
Apfelmus apple purée
Apfelsaft apple juice
Apfelstrudel apple strudel
Apfeltasche apple turnover

Apfelwein cider
Artischocken artichokes
Auberginen aubergines
Auflauf (baked) pudding or omelette
Aufschnitt sliced cold cuts
Austern oysters
Baiser meringue
Balkansalat cabbage and pepper salad
Bauernfrühstück bacon and potato omelette
Bechamelkartoffeln sliced potatoes in
  creamy sauce
Bedienung service
Beilagen side dishes
Bier beer
Bismarckheringe filleted pickled herring
Blätterteig puff pastry
Blumenkohl cauliflower
Blumenkohlsuppe cauliflower soup
Bockwurst large frankfurter
Bohneneintopf bean stew
Bouillon clear soup
Bouletten meat balls
Braten roast meat
Bratheringe (pickled) fried herring *(served
  cold)*
Bratkartoffeln fried potatoes
Bratwurst grilled pork sausage
Brot bread
Brühwurst large frankfurter
Bückling smoked red herring
Bunte Platte mixed platter
Buttercremetorte cream cake
Champignons mushrooms
Chicoree chickory
Chinakohl Chinese cabbage
Cordon bleu veal cordon bleu
Currywurst mit Pommes frites curried
  pork sausage with chips
Deutsches Beefsteak mince patty
Eier eggs

Eierpfannkuchen pancake
Eingelegte Heringe pickled herrings
Eintopf stew
Eis ice
Eisbecher sundae
Eisbein knuckles of pork
Eissplittertorte cake with fine chips of ice
Entenbraten roast duck
Erbsensuppe pea soup
Erdbeertorte strawberry cake
Fasan pheasant
Feldsalat lamb's lettuce
Fischfilet filleted fish
Fischstäbchen fish fingers
Fleischbrühe bouillon
Fleischkäse meat loaf
Fleischklößchen meat ball(s)
Fleischsalat diced meat salad with
  mayonnaise
Forelle blau trout au bleu
Forelle Müllerin (Art) trout with butter and
  lemon (breaded)
Frikadelle rissole
Fruchtsaft fruit juice
Frühlingsrolle spring roll
Gabelrollmops rolled-up pickled herring,
  rollmops
Gänsebraten roast goose
Gänseleberpastete goose liver pâté
Gebäck pastries, cakes
Geflügel poultry
Geflügelleberragout chicken liver ragout
Gefüllte Paprika stuffed peppers
Gefüllte Kalbsbrust stuffed breast of veal
Gekochter Schinken boiled ham
Gemischter Salat mixed salad
Gemüse vegetable(s)
Gericht dish
Geschnetzeltes strips of meat in thick sauce
Getränke beverages

Gewürze spices
Goldbarsch type of perch
Götterspeise jelly
Grießpudding semolina pudding
Grüne Bohnen French beans
Grünkohl (curly) kale
Gulasch goulash
Gulaschsuppe goulash soup
Gurkensalat cucumber salad
Hackfleisch mince
Hähnchen chicken
Halbes Hähnchen half chicken
Halbtrocken medium-dry
Hammelbraten roast mutton
Hasenpfeffer jugged hare
Hauptspeisen main courses
Hausfrauenart home-made-style
Hausmacher (Art) home-made-style
Heilbutt halibut
Heringssalat herring salad
Himmel und Erde potato and apple purée
  with blood/liver sausage
Hirschbraten roast venison
Hühnerbrühe chicken broth
Hühnerfrikassee chicken fricassee
Hummer lobster
Jägerschnitzel pork with mushrooms
Kabeljau cod
Kaffee coffee
Kaiserschmarren sugared pancake with
  raisins
Kalbsbraten roast veal
Kalbshaxe leg of veal
Kalbsmedaillons small veal fillets
Kalte Platte cold meal
Kalter Braten cold meat
Kaltschale cold sweet soup
Karpfen carp
Kartoffelbrei potato purée
Kartoffelklöße potato dumplings

Kartoffelknödel potato dumplings
Kartoffelpuffer potato fritters
Kartoffelpüree potato purée
Kartoffelsalat potato salad
Käsekuchen cheesecake
Käseplatte selection of cheeses
Kasseler Rippenspeer salted rib of pork
Kassler smoked and braised pork chop
Kieler Sprotten smoked sprats
Klare Brühe clear soup
Klöße dumplings
Knacker frankfurter(s)
Knoblauchbrot garlic bread
Knochenschinken ham on the bone
Knödel dumplings
Kohl cabbage
Kohlrouladen stuffed cabbage leaves
Kompott stewed fruit
Königinpastete chicken vol-au-vent
Königsberger Klopse meatballs in caper
  sauce
Kopfsalat lettuce
Kotelett chop
Krabbencocktail prawn cocktail
Kraftbrühe beef tea
Kräutersauce herb sauce
Krautsalat coleslaw
Kuchen cake
Labskaus meat, fish and potato stew
Lachs salmon
Lachsschinken smoked rolled fillet of ham
Lammrücken saddle of lamb
Lauchsuppe leek soup
Leberkäse baked pork and beef loaf
Leberknödel liver dumplings
Leberpastete liver pâté
Leipziger Allerlei mixed vegetables
Likör liqueur
Limonade lemonade
Linseneintopf lentil stew

....

Markklößchen marrow dumplings
Matjes(hering) young herring
Medaillons small fillets
Meeresfrüchte seafood
Meerrettichsauce horseradish sauce
Mehrwertsteuer VAT
Milch milk
Milchreis rice pudding
Mineralwasser (sparkling) mineral water
Möhren carrots
Muscheln mussels
Nach Art des Hauses home-made
Nach Hausfrauenart home-made
Nachspeisen desserts
Nierenragout kidney ragout
Nudelsalat noodle salad
Obstsalat fruit salad
Ochsenschwanzsuppe oxtail soup
Orangensaft orange juice
Paprikasalat pepper salad
Pastete vol-au-vent
Pellkartoffeln potatoes boiled in their jackets
Petersilienkartoffeln potatoes with parsley
Pfannkuchen pancake(s)
Pichelsteiner Topf vegetable stew with diced
  beef
Pilze mushrooms
Pilzsoße mushroom sauce
Pommes frites French fried potatoes
Porree leek
Potthast braised beef with sauce
Preßkopf brawn
Prinzeßbohnen unsliced runner beans
Püree (potato) purée
Putenschenkel turkey leg
Räucheraal smoked eel
Räucherhering kipper, smoked herring
Rehbraten roast venison
Reibekuchen potato waffles
Reisauflauf rice pudding

Reissalat rice salad
Rheinischer Sauerbraten braised beef
Rinderbraten pot roast
Rindfleischsuppe beef broth
Rindsroulade beef olive
Rippchen spare-rib
Risi-Pisi rice and peas
Rohkostplatte selection of salads
Rollmops rolled-up pickled herring, rollmops
Rosé rosé
Rosenkohl Brussels sprouts
Rostbraten roast
Rösti fried potatoes and onions
Röstkartoffeln fried potatoes
Rotbarsch type of perch
Rotkohl red cabbage
Rotwein red wine
Rührei mit Speck scrambled egg with bacon
Russische Eier egg mayonnaise
Sahne cream
Sahnesoße cream sauce
Salatplatte selection of salads
Salzheringe pickled herrings
Salzkartoffeln boiled potatoes
Sauerbraten marinaded potroast
Sauerkraut white cabbage, finely chopped and
   pickled
Schaschlik (shish-)kebab
Schellfisch haddock
Schillerlocken smoked haddock rolls
Schinken ham
Schinkenröllchen rolled ham
Schlachtplatte selection of fresh sausages
Schlagsahne whipped cream
Schmorbraten pot roast
Schnitzel cutlet
Scholle plaice
Schwarzwälder Kirschtorte Black Forest
   cherry gâteau
Schwarzwurzeln salsifies

Schweinebraten roast pork
Schweinefleisch pork
Schweinshaxe knuckle of pork
Seelachs pollack *(fish)*
Seezunge sole
Sekt sparkling wine, champagne
Selleriesalat celery salad
Semmelknödel bread dumplings
Senfsauce mustard sauce
Serbisches Reisfleisch diced pork, onions,
  tomatoes and rice
Spanferkel sucking pig
Spargelcremesuppe cream of asparagus soup
Spätzle home-made noodles
Speckknödel bacon dumplings
Speisekarte menu
Spiegeleier fried eggs
Spießbraten joint roasted on a spit
Spinat spinach
Spitzkohl white cabbage
Sprudel(wasser) mineral water
Stollen pastry loaf, filled with nuts and fruit,
  traditionally eaten at Christmas
Suppen soups
Sülze brawn
Süß sweet
Süßspeisen sweet dishes
Szegediner Gulasch goulash with pickled
  cabbage
Tafelwasser (still) mineral water
Tafelwein table wine
Tagesgericht dish of the day
Tageskarte menu of the day
Tagessuppe soup of the day
Tee tea
Thunfisch tuna
Tomatensuppe tomato soup
Törtchen tart(s)
Torte gâteau
Trocken dry

Truthahn turkey
Ungarischer Gulasch Hungarian Goulash
Verlorene Eier poached eggs
Vom Kalb veal
Vom Rind beef
Vom Schwein pork
Vorspeisen hors d'oeuvres, starters
Waldorfsalat salad with celery, apples and
  walnuts
Wasser water
Weinbrand brandy
Weißkohl white cabbage
Weißwein white wine
Weißwurst veal sausage
Wiener Schnitzel veal in breadcrumbs
Wild game
Wirsing savoy cabbage
Würstchen frankfurter(s)
Wurstsalat sausage salad
Zigeunerschnitzel pork with peppers and
  relishes
Zucchini courgettes
Zuckererbsen mange-tout peas
Zwiebelsuppe onion soup
Zwiebeltorte onion tart
Zwischengerichte entrées

In Greece, eating places range from the **OYZEPI** *[oozeri]* — a simple snack bar — to the **ΕΣΤΙΑ-ΤΟΡΙΟΝ** *[estee-atoree-on]* — a formal restaurant serving full meals. You will find genuine Greek cuisine in most eating places, but especially in villages and on the smaller islands.

It is the custom for water and bread to be brought to the table as soon as you arrive at a restaurant (before you order) and for the customer to visit the kitchen to see what's available to eat. By law, restaurants and bars close at 3 a.m. In Greece, children are allowed into licensed restaurants.

The most distinctive Greek wine is **ρετσίνα** *[retseena]* (flavoured with pine resin) — try it in an *oozeri* — a bar which serves **ούζο** *[oozo]* (an aniseed-flavoured spirit) and beer or wine with a selection of savoury snacks (**μεζέδες** *[mezethes]*). These can consist of cheese, cucumber, octopus, olives, cod roe dip (**ταραμοσαλάτα** *[taramosalata]*) and various local specialities.

Whether it's a full meal you want or just a drink, try the traditional Greek **TABEPNA** *[tav-erna]*. *Tavernas* tend to specialize in either fish, seafood or meat dishes. Many are near the sea, and you can often have your meal out-of-doors overlooking the harbour. Draught wine is ordered by weight not volume, so be sure to ask for a kilo not a litre!

If you feel like a coffee, you should go to a **ΖΑΧΑ-ΡΟΠΛΑΣΤΕΙΟ** *[zakharoplastio]*, which is a café serving delicious cakes and gâteaux. This type of café is popular with families, but if you are looking for something different, try a **ΚΑΦΕΝΕΙΟ** *[kafenio]* — a traditional coffee house serving

Greek coffee, _oo_zo, _mezethes_ and sweets, where Greek men meet to play cards or backgammon.

ORDERING

In the pronunciation that follows, _TH_ (θ) should be pronounced as in 'theatre' and _th_ (δ) as in 'the'.

excuse me!
παρακαλώ!
[_parakalo_]

can I order please?
μπορώ να παραγγείλω;
[_boro na parangeelo_]

one . . ./two . . .
ένα (μία)/δύο . . .
[_ena (meea)/thee-o_]

that's for me/him
αυτό είναι γιά μένα/αυτόν
[_afto eene ya mena/afton_]

can I see the menu again?
μπορώ να δω τον κατάλογο πάλι;
[_boro na tho ton katalogo palee_]

can you bring me another red wine/beer?
μπορείτε να μου φέρετε ένα ακόμη κόκκινο κρασί/μία μπύρα;
[_boreete na moo ferete ena akomee kokkeeno krassee/mee-a beera_]

could I have the bill please?
το λογαριασμό, παρακαλώ
[_to logaree-asmo parakalo_]

if the waiter/waitress says:
σας άρεσε το φαγητό;
[sas aresse to fageeto]
did you enjoy your meal?

you could say:
ναι ευχαριστώ
[ne efkhareesto]
yes, thank you

SOME BASIC WORDS

beer μία μπύρα *[mee-a beera]*
bottle ένα μπουκάλι *[ena bookalee]*
brandy ένα μπράντι *[ena brandee]*
bread ψωμί *[psomee]*
coffee ένα καφές *[ena kafess]*
cup ένα φλιτζάνι *[ena fleedzanee]*
dry ξερό *[ksero]*
fork ένα πηρούνι *[ena peeroonee]*
fruit juice ένα χυμό *[ena kheemo]*
glass ένα ποτήρι *[poteeree]*
gin and tonic ένα τζην με τόνιχ *[ena gin me tonik]*
half-bottle μισό μπουκάλι *[meesso bookalee]*
hot chocolate μία ζεστή σοχολάτα *[mee-a zestee sokolata]*
ice πάγος *[pagoss]*
knife ένα μαχαίρι *[ena makheree]*
lager μία μπύρα *[mee-a beera]*
lemonade μία λεμονάδα *[mee-a lemonatha]*
milk γάλα *[gala]*
mineral water μεταλλικό νερό *[metalleeko nero]*
mineral water *(fizzy)* μεταλλικό νερό με ανθρακιχό *[metalleeko nero me anтнrakeeko]*
napkin πετσέτα φαγητού *[pesteta fagtoo]*
orange juice ένα χυμό πορτοχαλιού *[ena kheemo portokalee-oo]*

pepper πιπέρι *[peeperi]*
red wine κόκκινο κρασί *[kokkeeno krassee]*
rose ροζέ *[rozay]*
salt αλάτι *[alatee]*
spoon ένα κουτάλι *[ena kootalee]*
sugar ζάχαρη *[zakharee]*
sweet γλυκό *[gleeko]*
tea ένα τσάι *[ena tsa-ee]*
water νερό *[nero]*
whisky ένα ουίσκι *[ena weeskee]*
white wine άσπρο κρασί *[aspro krassee]*

UNDERSTANDING THE MENU

COOKING METHODS, SAUCES ETC

αυγολέμονο *[avgolemono]* egg and lemon sauce
βραστό *[vrasto]* boiled, stewed
γεμιστά *[yemeesta]* stuffed *(usually with rice and/or minced meat)*
καπνιστό *[kapneesto]* smoked
κοκκινιστό *[kokeeneesto]* in tomato sauce
κρασάτο *[krassato]* cooked in wine sauce
λαδερά *[lathera]* in olive oil and tomato sauce
με λαδολέμονο *[me latholemono]* with olive oil and lemon dressing
με σάλτσα *[me saltsa]* with sauce *(usually tomato sauce)*
πλακί *[plakee]* baked in tomato sauce
στο φούρνο *[sto foorno]* baked in the oven
σκορδαλιά *[skorthalee-a]* thick garlic sauce
σωτέ *[sotay]* sautéed
τηγανητό *[teeganeeto]* fried
της κατσαρόλας *[teess katsarolass]* baked in a casserole
της σούβλας *[teess soovlass]* roasted on a spit
της σχάρας *[teess skharass]* charcoal-grilled
τουρσί *[toors-ee]* pickled
ψητό *[pseeto]* 1. charcoal-grilled; 2. roasted

OPEKTIKA *[ORETEEKA]* STARTERS

γαρίδες *[gareethess]* prawns
ελιές *[elee-ess]* olives
καλαμαράκια *[kalamarakee-a]* squid
κεφτέδες *[keftethess]* meat balls
κοκορέτσι *[kokoretsee]* spit-roasted liver and
   innards
κολοκυθάκια τηγανητά *[kolokeeтнakee-a
   teeganeeta]* fried courgettes
κρεατόπιτα *[kre-atopeeta]* minced meat in filo
   pastry
μελιτζανοσαλάτα *[meleedzanosalata]* puréed
   aubergine dip
μύδια *[meethee-a]* mussels
μυαλά *[mee-ala]* brains
ντολμαδάκια *[dolmathakee-a]* vine leaves
   stuffed with minced meat, rice and herbs
ντολμάδες *[dolmathess]* vine or cabbage leaves
   stuffed with minced meat and/or rice
σαγανάκι *[saganakee]* fried cheese and egg
σαρδέλλες *[sartheless]* sardines
σουπιές *[soopee-ess]* cuttlefish
σπανακόπιτα *[spanakopeetta]* spinach in filo
   pastry
στρείδια *[streethee-a]* oysters
ταραμάς *[taramass]* cod roe
ταραμοσαλάτα *[taramosalata]* cod roe dip
τζατζίκι *[tzadzeekee]* cucumber, yogurt and
   garlic dip
τόννος *[tonnoss]* tuna
τυρόπιτα *[teeropeeta]* cheese and egg in filo
   pastry
θαλασσινά *[тнalasseena]* sea food
χταπόδι *[khtapothee]* octopus
χωριάτικη σαλάτα *[khoreeateekee
   salata]* 'country' salad consisting of tomatoes,
   cucumber, feta cheese, peppers, olives and
   boiled eggs with an oil and vinegar dressing

ΣΟΥΠΕΣ *[SOOPESS]* SOUPS

αυγολέμονο *[avgolemono]* chicken broth with
lemon and egg
κακαβιά *[kakavee-a]* mixed fish soup
μαγειρίτσα *[mayeereetsa]* traditional lamb soup
*(served on the Saturday night before Easter
Sunday)*
πατσάς *[patzass]* lamb's intestines soup
φακές *[fakess]* lentil soup
φασολάδα *[fassolatha]* bean soup with celery,
carrots and tomatoes
ψαρόσουπα *[psarossoopa]* fish soup

ΚΡΕΑΤΙΚΑ *[KREE-ATEEKA]*

MEAT DISHES

αρνάκι *[arnakee]* lamb
αρνάκι εξοχικό *[arnakee eksokheeko]* leg of
lamb baked in greaseproof paper
αρνάκι με μπάμιες *[arnakee me bamee-ess]* lamb and okra stew
αρνάκι με πατάτες στο φούρνο *[arnakee me
patatess sto foorno]* roast lamb and potatoes
αρνάκι τας κεμπάμπ *[arnakee tass kebap]* lamb
in tomato sauce
αρνάκι της σούβλας *[arnakee teess
soovlass]* lamb roast on the spit
αρνάκι φρικασέ με μαρούλια *[arnakee
freekassay me maroolee-a]* lamb and lettuce
with a thick white sauce
αρνί *[arnee]* mutton, lamb
βωδινό *[votheeno]* beef
γαλοπούλα *[galopoola]* turkey
γαρδούμπα *[garthooba]* rolled lamb offal on a
spit
γιουβαρλάκια *[yoovarlakee-a]* minced meat or
meat balls, rice and seasoning in a sauce
γιουβέτσι *[yoovetsee]* roast lamb with pasta
κεφτέδες *[keftethess]* meatballs

κοκορέτσι *[kokoretsee]* rolled lamb offal on a spit

κολοκυθάκια με κρέας *[kolokeeтнakee-a me kre-ass]* courgettes and beef stew

κότα *[kota]* chicken

κοτόπουλο *[kotopoolo]* chicken

κουνέλι *[koonelee]* rabbit

κρέας *[kre-ass]* meat *(usually beef)*

λαγός στιφάδο *[lagoss steefatho]* hare and shallot stew

λαχανοντολμάδες *[lakhanodolmathess]* cabbage leaves stuffed with minced meat and rice

μακαρόνια με χιμά *[makaronee-a me keema]* spaghetti bolognaise

μακαρόνια παστίτσιο *[makaronee-a pasteetsee-o]* layers of pasta and mince or cheese topped with white sauce

μελιτζάνες μουσακά *[meleedzaness moossaka]* moussaka — layers of aubergine and mince topped with white sauce

μοσχάρι *[moskharee]* 1. veal; 2. tender beef

μοσχάρι με μελιτζάνες *[moskharee me meleedzaness]* veal and aubergine stew

μοσχάρι με φασολάχια *[moskharee me fassolakee-a]* veal and green beans

μοσχάρι ψητό *[moskharee pseeto]* pot-roast of veal

μουσακάς *[moossakass]* moussaka — layers of vegetables and minced meat topped with white sauce

μπριζόλες *[breezoless]* 1. chops; 2. steaks

μπριζόλες χοιρινές στη σχάρα *[breezoless kheereeness stee skhara]* pork chops grilled over charcoal

μπιφτέχι *[beeftekee]* hamburger

πατσάς *[patsass]* tripe

σουβλάχια *[soovlakee-a]* meat grilled on a skewer and served in pitta bread

στιφάδο *[steefatho]* hare or rabbit stew with onions

συκώτι ψητό *[seekoti pseeto]* liver grilled over charcoal
χοιρινό *[kheereeno]* pork

ΘΑΛΑΣΣΙΝΑ *[THALASSEENA]*

SEAFOOD

αστακός *[astakoss]* lobster
γαρίδες *[gareethess]* prawns
γαριδοπίλαφο *[gareethopeel-afo]* prawns with rice cooked in butter
γλώσσα *[glossa]* sole
καβούρια *[kavooree-a]* boiled crab
καλαμαράκια *[kalamarakee-a]* fried baby squid
καραβίδες *[karaveethess]* king prawns
λυθρίνι *[leeτнreenee]* red snapper
μπακαλιάρος *[bakalee-aross]* cod
μπαρμπούνια *[barboonee-a]* red mullet
μύδια *[eethee-a]* mussels
ξιφίας *[kseefee-ass]* swordfish
σουπιές με σπανάκι *[soopee-ess me spanakee]* cuttlefish and spinach stew
τσιπούρα *[tseepoora]* sea bream
ψάρια *[psaree-a]* fish

ΧΟΡΤΑΡΙΚΑ *[KHORTAREEKA]*

VEGETABLES

αγγουράκια *[agoorakyee-a]* cucumbers
αρακάς *[arakass]* peas
κολοκυθάκια *[kolokeeτнakee-a]* courgettes
κολοκυθάκια γιαχνί *[kolokeeτнakee-a yakhnee]* courgettes in a tomato sauce
κουνουπίδι *[koonoopeethee]* cauliflower
κρεμμυδάκια *[kremmeeτнakee-a]* spring onions
κρεμμύδια *[kremmeethee-a]* onions
λαχανικά *[lakhaneeka]* vegetables
λάχανο *[lakhano]* cabbage
μανιτάρια *[maneetaree-a]* mushrooms

....

μελιτζάνες *[meleedzaness]* aubergines
μελιτζάνες παπουτσάχια *[meleedzaness papootsakee-a]* stuffed aubergines
μπάμιες *[bamee-ess]* okra
μπάμιες λαδερές *[bamee-ess latheress]* okra in olive oil and tomato sauce
μπριάμι *[bree-amee]* ratatouille — tomato, peppers, aubergine and courgette stew
ντομάτες *[domatess]* tomatoes
ντομάτες γεμιστές *[domatess yemeestess]* stuffed tomatoes
πατάτες *[patatess]* potatoes
πατάτες γιαχνί *[patatess yakhnee]* potatoes and onions in tomato sauce
πατάτες ριγανάτες στο φούρνο *[patatess reeganatess sto foorno]* oven-baked potatoes with oregano
πιπεριά *[peeperee-a]* green pepper
πιπεριές γεμιστές *[peeperee-ess yemeestess]* stuffed green peppers
σέλινο *[seleeno]* celery
σκόρδο *[skortho]* garlic
φάβα *[fava]* split peas
φασολάκια *[fassolakee-a]* green beans
φασολάκια λαδερά *[fassolakee-a lathera]* green beans in olive oil and tomato sauce
φασόλια *[fassolee-a]* beans
φασόλια γίγαντες *[fassolee-a yeegandess]* large dried beans in tomato sauce

ΖΥΜΑΡΙΚΑ *[ZEEMAREEKA]*

PASTA AND RICE

ατζέμ πιλάφι *[atzem peelafee]* rice pilaff
λαζάνια *[lazanee-a]* tagliatelle
μακαρόνια *[makaronee-a]* pasta
πιλάφι *[peelafee]* rice

ΤΥΡΙΑ ΚΑΙ ΑΥΓΑ [TEEREE-A KE AVGA]
CHEESE AND EGGS

ανθότυρο [anτHoteero] aromatic cheese
αυγά μάτια [avga matee-a] fried eggs
αυγά μελάτα [avga melata] soft-boiled eggs
αυγά σφιχτά [avga sfeekhta] hard-boiled eggs
κασέρι [kasseree] mild, Cheddar-type cheese
κεφαλοτύρι [kefaloteeree] salty, hard cheese
μανούρι [manooree] hard cheese
φέτα [feta] soft white cheese

ΓΛΥΚΑ [GLEEKA] SWEETS

αμυγδαλωτά [ameegthalota] almond pastries
γαλακτομπούρεκο [galaktobooreko] thin, sweet
  filo pastry with custard filling
γλυκό βύσσινο [gleeko veesseeno] candied
  cherries in syrup
γλυκό σύκο [gleeko seeko] candied figs in syrup
καταΐφι [kada-eefee] shredded and rolled filo
  pastry in syrup
κουραμπιέδες [koorabee-ethess] shortbread
λουκουμάδες [lookoomathess] fried doughnuts
  in honey
λουκούμια [lookoomee-a] Turkish delight
μελομακάρονα [melomakarona] fritters coated
  with nuts and syrup
μπαχλαβάς [baklavass] baklava (filo pastry with
  nuts and syrup)
μπουγάτσα [boogatsa] puff pastry with various
  fillings
παγωτό [pagoto] ice cream
πάστα [pasta] cake
πορτοκάλι [portokalee] orange, boiled and
  sugared
ρυζόγαλο [reezogalo] rice pudding
τσουρέκι [tsoorekee] light sponge
χαλβάς [khalvass] sweet made from sesame
  seeds nuts and honey

ΦΡΟΥΤΑ ΚΑΙ ΞΗΡΟΙ ΚΑΡΠΟΙ
[FROOTA KE KSEEREE KARPEE]
FRUIT AND NUTS

αμύγδαλα *[ameegthala]* almonds
αχλάδια *[akhlathee-a]* pears
βερύκοκα *[vereekoka]* apricots
ξηροί καρποί *[kseeree karpee]* 1. nuts; 2. dried fruit
καρπούζι *[karpoozee]* watermelon
κεράσια *[kerassee-a]* cherries
μήλα *[meela]* apples
πεπόνι *[peponee]* melon
πορτοκάλι *[portokalee]* orange
ροδάκινα *[rothakeena]* peaches
σταφύλια *[stafeelee-a]* grapes
σύκα *[seeka]* figs
φράουλες *[fra-ooles]* strawberries
φυστίκια Αιγίνης *[feesteekee-a E-yeeneess]* pistachios

ΠΟΤΑ *[POTA]* DRINKS

άσπρο κρασί *[aspro krassee]* white wine
γαλλικός καφές *[galeekoss kafess]* filter coffee
γλυκό κρασί *[gleeko]* sweet wine
ελληνικός καφές *[eleeneekoss kafess]* Greek coffee *(very strong black coffee)*
καφές βαρύς γλυκός *[kafess vareess gleekoss]* sweet Greek coffee
καφές με γάλα *[kafess me gala]* coffee with milk
κρασί μαυροδάφνη *[krassee mavrothafnee]* sweet red wine
κρασί ρετσίνα *[krassee retseena]* retsina *(wine flavoured with pine resin)*
μεταλλικό νερό *[metalleeko nero]* mineral water
μπύρα *[beera]* beer, lager
νέσκαφε *[neskafe]* instant coffee
νέσκαφε φραπέ *[neskafe frape]* iced coffee

ούζο *[oozo]* ouzo *(liquor distilled from grapeskins and flavoured with aniseed)*

πορτοκάλι χυμός *[portokalee kheemoss]* fresh orange juice

τσάι *[tsa-ee]* tea

κόκκινο κρασί *[kokkeeno krassee]* red wine

THE best food in Italy is the regional fare, offered by the majority of restaurants. Ethnic restaurants are rare and quite expensive. There are also **pizzerie**, serving a wide range of **pizze**. The typical meal you would order in a restaurant consists of a first course — generally a pasta or rice (**risotto**) dish and a main course — meat or fish, with vegetables or salads served separately; the dessert is often just fruit or is replaced by coffee. Bread and breadsticks (**grissini**) are put on the table as you sit down and wine is brought immediately after. Some restaurants specialize in **antipasti** (starters) — pickled fish, salami, salads, pickled mushrooms etc. Throughout the country there is a tremendous variety of foods on offer, therefore the restaurant menus will look quite different.

Wines vary from region to region and it is always worth asking for the **vino della casa** (house wine, usually served in a carafe), which is often cheaper and more suited to the local food than the bottled, branded types. In restaurants, Italians generally order mineral water (fizzy and still are both readily available) rather than tap water.

Prices also vary quite a lot, but all restaurants must clearly show the price list outside the establishment. Service and VAT (**IVA**) are normally included, but a small tip is generally expected.

ORDERING

excuse me!
scusi!
[sk<u>oo</u>zee]

can I order please?
vorrei ordinare?
[vor-ray ordeenaray]

one . . ./two . . .
un (uno/una) . . ./due . . .
[oon (oono/oona) . . ./doo-ay]

that's for me/him
è per me/per lui
[eh pair may/pair loo-ee]

can I see the menu again?
posso vedere il menu un'altra volta?
[pos-so vedairay eel menoo oon altra volta]

can you bring me another red wine/beer
mi può portare dell'altro vino rosso/dell'altra
birra
[mee pwo portaray dail-laltro veeno ros-so/dail-laltra beer-ra]

could I have the bill please?
mi dà il conto, per piacere?
[mee dah eel conto, pair pee-achairay]

if the waiter/waitress says:
 ha mangiato bene?
 [a manjee-ato benay]
 did you enjoy your meal?

you could reply:
 si, benissimo
 [see benees-seemo]
 yes, thank you

SOME BASIC WORDS

beer una birra *[oona beer-ra]*
bottle una bottiglia *[oona botee-lya]*
brandy un brandy

....

bread del pane *[del p*a*nay]*
coffee un caffè *[oon kaf-f*e*h]*
cup una tazza *[*oo*na t*a*tza]*
dry secco
fork una forchetta *[*oo*na fork*e*t-ta]*
fruit juice un succo di frutta *[oon s*oo*k-ko dee
    fr*oo*ta]*
glass un bicchiere *[oon beek-y*a*iray]*
gin and tonic un gin e tonica *[oon jeen ay
    ton*eeka*]*
half-bottle una mezza bottiglia *[*oo*na m*e*tza
    bot*ee*-lya]*
hot chocolate una cioccolata calda *[*oo*na chok-
    kol*a*ta k*a*lda]*
ice ghiacciolo *[g-yach*o*lo]*
knife un coltello *[oon kolt*a*ylo]*
lager una birra chiara *[*oo*na b*ee*r-ra kee-*a*ra]*
lemonade una limonata *[*oo*na leemon*a*ta]*
milk latte *[l*a*t-tay]*
mineral water acqua minerale *[*a*kwa
    meenair*a*lay]*
mineral water (fizzy) acqua minerale gasata
    *[*a*kwa meenair*a*lay gas*a*ta]*
napkin un tovagliolo *[oon toval-y*o*lo]*
orange juice un succo d'arancia *[oon s*oo*k-ko
    dar*a*ncha]*
pepper pepe *[p*e*pay]*
red wine vino rosso *[v*ee*no r*o*sso]*
rosé rosé *[ros*a*y]*
salt sale *[s*a*lay]*
spoon un cucchiaio *[oon kook-y*a*-yo]*
sugar zucchero *[tz*oo*k-kairo]*
sweet dolce *[d*o*lchay]*
tea tè *[teh]*
water acqua (naturale) *[*a*kwa natoor*a*lay]*
whisky un whisky
white wine vino bianco *[v*ee*no bee-*a*nko]*

UNDERSTANDING THE MENU

abbacchio alla romana Roman-style spring lamb

acciuga fresh anchovy

acciughe sott'olio anchovies in oil

acqua minerale gasata sparkling mineral water

acqua minerale (non gasata) still mineral water

affettato misto assorted cold, sliced meats

affogato poached

affogato al caffè ice cream with hot espresso coffee

agnello lamb

ai ferri grilled

albicocche apricots

al burro cooked in butter

al cartoccio baked in foil

al formaggio with cheese

al forno baked or roasted in the oven

alice fresh anchovy

alla brace charcoal-grilled

alla campagnola country-style

alla casalinga home-made

alla coque soft-boiled *(egg)*

alla griglia grilled

all'agro dressed with oil and lemon juice

allo spiedo spit-roasted

al mattone baked in a brick *(usually chicken)*

al pomodoro with tomato

ananas pineapple

anatra duck

anatra all'arancia duck à l'orange

anguria water melon

antipasti starters

antipasti misti mixed hors d'oeuvres

aragosta lobster

aranciata orangeade

aringa herring

arista di maiale al forno roast chine of pork
arrosto roast
arrosto di vitello roast veal
asparagi asparagus
bavarese ice-cream cake made from milk, eggs and fresh cream
Bel Paese soft, full fat cheese
besciamella white sauce
bevande drinks
bignè profiteroles
birra beer
birra chiara lager
birra grande ($\frac{1}{2}$ litro) large beer
birra piccola ($\frac{1}{4}$ litro) small beer
birra scura dark beer, bitter
bistecca (di manzo) beef steak
bistecca ai ferri grilled steak
bistecca alla fiorentina grilled T-bone steak
bistecca alla pizzaiola grilled steak with tomato sauce
bollito boiled
bollito misto boiled meats with vegetables
branzino sea bass
brasato braised beef with herbs
bresaola dried, salted beef eaten cold
brodo di pollo chicken broth
budino pudding
bufalina buffalo milk cheese like mozzarella
caciotta tender, medium fat cheese
caffè coffee
caffellatte half coffee, half hot milk
caffè lungo weak espresso coffee
caffè ristretto strong espresso coffee
calamaro squid
calamari in umido squid in wine, garlic and tomato sauce
calzone folded pizza with tomato and mozzarella or ricotta cheese inside
cannelloni al forno rolls of egg pasta filled with meat and baked in the oven

cappelletti pasta parcels with meat filling
cappone capon
capretto al forno roast kid
carciofi artichokes
carne meat
carré di maiale al forno roast pork loin
cassata siciliana Sicilian ice-cream cake with
  glacé fruit, chocolate and ricotta cheese
castagne chestnuts
cavoletti di Bruxelles Brussels sprouts
cavolfiore cauliflower
cervella al burro calf's brains cooked in
  butter
cervo venison
cetrioli cucumber
cicoria chicory
ciliege cherries
cime di rapa very small leafy broccoli
cioccolata chocolate
cipolle onions
cocktail di gamberetti prawn cocktail
coniglio arrosto roast rabbit
coniglio in salmí jugged rabbit
contorni vegetables
coperto cover charge
costata (di manzo) beef entrecôte
cotechino spiced pork sausage
cotoletta alla milanese veal cutlet in
  breadcrumbs
cotoletta alla valdostana veal cutlet with
  ham and cheese cooked in breadcrumbs
cozze mussels
crema al cioccolato chocolate cream pudding
crema di piselli cream of pea soup
crescenza fresh, full fat runny cheese
crocchette di patate potato rissoles
crostata di frutta fruit tart
dentice al forno baked type of sea bream
dolci cakes, gâteaux
fagiano pheasant

....

fagioli beans
fagiolini long, green beans
faraona guinea fowl
fettuccine ribbon-shaped pasta
filetti di ... ... fillet of
filetto fillet of beef
filetto al sangue rare fillet of beef
filetto ben cotto well-done fillet of beef
filetto medio medium-done fillet of beef
finocchi al forno fennel with cheese, browned
   in the oven
finocchio fennel
fontina soft cheese used for cooking
formaggi misti assorted cheeses
fragole strawberries
frittata type of omelette
fritto fried
fritto misto meat, vegetables or fish fried in
   batter
frittura di pesce variety of fried fish
frutta fruit
frutta secca dried nuts and raisins
frutti di mare seafood
funghi mushrooms
funghi trifolati mushrooms fried in garlic and
   parsley
gamberetti prawns
gamberi crayfish
gamberoni king prawns
gelato ice cream
gnocchi small flour and potato dumplings
gorgonzola strong, soft blue cheese
grancevola spiny spider crab
granchio crab
grigliato grilled
grigliata mista mixed grill *(meat or fish)*
grissini thin, crisp breadsticks
in brodo in a soup
in camicia poached *(egg)*
in carpione soused

in crosta en croûte, in pastry
indivia endive
insalata salad
insalata di mare seafood salad
insalata di pomodori tomato salad
insalata di riso rice salad
insalata mista mixed salad
insalata russa Russian salad
insalata verde green salad
in salsa in a sauce
in umido stewed
involtini stuffed rolls *(of meat, pastry etc.)*
lamponi raspberries
lasagne al forno sheets of pasta baked with
  layers of tomato, mince and cheese
lattuga lettuce
legumi pulses
lenticchie lentils
lepre in salmì jugged hare
limone lemon
lingua tongue
macedonia di frutta fruit salad
maiale pork
maionese mayonnaise
manzo beef
marroni chestnuts
mascarpone very rich clotted cream
mela apple
melanzane aubergines
melone melon
menta mint
meringata meringue pie
meringhe con panna meringues with fresh
  cream
merluzzo cod
messicani in gelatina beef olives in jelly
minestrone thick vegetable soup with rice
mirtilli bilberries
montone mutton
more mulberries, blackberries

....

mozzarella soft, sweet cheese made from
 buffalo's milk
mozzarella in carrozza slices of bread and
 mozzarella dipped in flour and fried
nasello hake
nocciole hazelnuts
noci walnuts
nodino (di vitello) veal chop
oca goose
olio oil
orata sea bream
ossobuco stewed shin of veal in wine and
 tomato sauce
ostriche oysters
paglia e fieno mixture of plain and green
 tagliatelle
paillard di manzo grilled slices of beef
pane bread
pane e coperto cover charge including bread
panino filled roll
parmigiana di melanzane baked layers of
 aubergines, tomato sauce, mozzarella and
 parmesan
parmigiano Parmesan cheese
pasta e fagioli thick soup with blended
 borlotti beans and pasta
pastina in brodo noodle soup
patate potatoes
patate fritte chips
pâté di fegato liver pâté
pecorino strong, hard ewe's milk cheese
penne pasta tubes *(larger than macaroni)*
penne ai quattro formaggi pasta tubes with
 sauce made from four cheeses
penne all'arrabbiata pasta tubes with tomato
 and chilli pepper sauce
peperonata green, red and yellow peppers
 stewed with tomatoes, onions and olive oil
peperoni peppers
peperoni ripieni stuffed peppers

pera pear
pesca peach
pesca melba peach melba
pesce fish
pesce al cartoccio fish baked in foil with
  herbs
pesce persico perch
pesce spada swordfish
piccione pigeon
pinzimonio mixed, whole, raw vegetables with
  oil and vinegar dressing
piselli peas
piselli al prosciutto fresh peas cooked in
  clear broth with butter, ham and basil
pizza Margherita pizza with tomato and
  mozzarella
pizza napoletana pizza with tomato,
  mozzarella and anchovies
pizza quattro stagioni pizza with tomato,
  mozzarella, ham, mushrooms and artichokes
pizzaiola slices of cooked beef in tomato sauce
  with oregano and anchovies
polenta cornmeal boiled in water with salt until
  firm and cut in slices
polenta pasticciata alternate layers of
  polenta, tomato sauce and cheese
pollo chicken
pollo alla cacciatora chicken in a wine, onion
  and tomato sauce
pollo alla diavola chicken pieces pressed and
  deep fried
pomodori tomatoes
pompelmo grapefruit
porchetta allo spiedo sucking pig roasted on
  the spit with herbs
porri leeks
prezzemolo parsley
primi piatti first courses
prosciutto cotto cooked ham
prosciutto crudo/di Parma dry-cured ham

prosciutto e melone dry-cured ham and melon
prugne plums
purè di patate mashed potatoes
quaglia quail
radicchio chicory
ragù sauce made with mince, tomatoes and
  diced vegetables
rapanelli radishes
ravioli small parcels of egg pasta stuffed with
  meat or cheese
ricotta soft, white, mild-flavoured cheese
riso rice
risotto rice cooked very slowly in clear broth
risotto ai funghi mushroom risotto
risotto alla milanese rice cooked in white
  wine and saffron with mushrooms and cheese
roast-beef all'inglese roast beef sliced very
  thinly and served cold with lemon
rognone trifolato small kidney pieces in
  garlic, oil and parsley
salmone affumicato smoked salmon
salsa di pomodoro tomato sauce
salsa tartara mayonnaise sauce with herbs,
  gherkins and capers
salsa verde sauce for meat made with
  chopped parsley and oil
salsiccia sausage
salsiccia di cinghiale wild boar's meat
  sausage
salsiccia di maiale pork sausage
saltato sautéed
saltimbocca alla romana veal escalopes with
  ham and sage
sarda sardine *(fresh)*
sarde ai ferri grilled sardines
scaloppine veal escalopes
scaloppine ai funghi veal escalopes with
  mushrooms
scaloppine al Marsala veal escalopes in
  Marsala

scamorza matured goat's milk cheese
scampi alla griglia grilled scampi
secondi piatti second courses
selvaggina game
semifreddo ice cream sponge
senape mustard
seppie cuttlefish
servizio compreso service charge included
servizio escluso not including service
 charge
sgombro mackerel
sogliola sole
sogliola alla mugnaia sole cooked in flour
 and butter
sorbetto sherbet, soft ice cream
spezzatino di vitello veal stew
spaghetti alla carbonara spaghetti with egg
 and bacon sauce
spaghetti alle vongole spaghetti with clams
spaghetti al ragù spaghetti with mince and
 tomato sauce
spaghetti al sugo spaghetti with meat sauce
specialita della casa chef's special
spezzatino di vitello veal stew
spiedini small pieces of assorted meats or fish
 cooked on a spit
spinaci spinach
stoccafisso dried cod
stracciatella clear soup with eggs and cheese
strapazzato scrambled
stufato stewed
succo d'arancia orange juice
svizzera hamburger
tacchino turkey
tacchino ripieno stuffed turkey
tagliatelle thin, flat strips of egg pasta
tagliatelle al pomodoro tagliatelle with
 tomato sauce
tagliatelle al ragù tagliatelle with mince and
 tomato sauce

....

tagliatelle alla bolognese tagliatelle with
  mince and tomato sauce
tagliolini thin noodles used in soup
taleggio mild, full fat cheese
tartufo round ice cream covered in cocoa or
  chocolate
tè tea
tiramisu coffee-soaked sponge with Marsala,
  cream and cocoa powder
tonno tuna
torta tart, flan
torta al formaggio cheese flan
torta di mele apple tart
torta gelato ice cream tart
tortellini small pasta parcels filled with pork
  loin, ham, parmesan and nutmeg
tortellini in brodo tortellini in clear broth
tortellini di magro small pasta parcels filled
  with cheese, parsley and chopped vegetables
trancio di pesce spada swordfish slice
trenette col pesto type of flat spaghetti with
  crushed basil, garlic, oil and cheese sauce
triglia mullet
trippa tripe
trota trout
uova alla coque boiled eggs
uova al tegamino con pancetta fried eggs
  and bacon
uova sode hard-boiled eggs
uva grapes
verdure vegetables
vino bianco white wine
vino da pasto/da tavola table wine
vino della casa house wine
vino rosso red wine
vitello veal
vongole clams
würstel frankfurter
zabaione frothy dessert made from beaten egg
  yolks, sugar and Marsala

zampone con lenticchie spicy pork sausage
  in the shape of a pig's trotter with lentils
zucca pumpkin
zucchine courgettes
zuccotto ice-cream cake with sponge, fresh
  cream and chocolate
zuppa di cipolle onion soup
zuppa di pesce fish soup
zuppa inglese trifle

In Oslo and the larger towns, there is a wide choice of attractive restaurants and eating establishments of a high standard. Traditional dishes are often served in folk museums or country restaurants. Fish dishes, and particularly shellfish, are popular and very good.

As fresh food was not always readily available in the olden days, traditional Norwegian dishes are often based on ingredients like salted, dried, cured or smoked meat and fish. **Fenalår** (cured mutton leg), **spekeskinke** (cured ham), **rakørret** (cured trout) and **gravlaks** (cured salmon) are typical Norwegian dishes. Soured cream is also used a lot in traditional dishes, for example in **rømmegrøt** (soured cream porridge) and **rømmevafler** (soured cream waffles).

Dinner is normally eaten early in Norway at about 4-5 p.m., but is often available in restaurants from that time onwards throughout the evening. Service charge of 10% and VAT (MOMS) at 20% are included in the menu prices and there is no obligation to give an extra tip. However, if people are particularly pleased with the meal or service, a tip of 5% of the total bill is often given.

Alcohol is by law not allowed to be served on Sundays and Holy Days (Christmas day etc). Spirits are only served from 3.p.m. to 11 p.m. although beer and aperitifs are available at other times. Norwegians mainly drink **pils** (lager) and **eksportøl** (strong lager).

ORDERING

excuse me!
unnskyld!
[ewnshewl]

can I order please?
kan jeg få bestille, takk?
[kan yɪ foh bestɪleh tak]

one .../two ...
en .../to ...
[ayn/toh]

that's for me/him
det er til meg/han
[deh ayr til mɪ/han]

can I see the menu again?
kan jeg få se menyen igjen?
[kan yɪ foh seh menee-en ee-yen]

can you bring me another red wine/beer?
kan du hente en rødvin/øl til?
[kan doo henta ayn ruhveen/ul til]

could I have the bill please?
kan jeg få regningen, takk?
[kan yɪ foh rayningen tak]

if the waiter/waitress says:
    smakte det?
    [smakteh deh]
    did it taste good?

you could reply:
    ja, takk
    [yah tak]
    yes, thank you

SOME BASIC WORDS

beer øl *[ul]*
bottle en flaske *[ayn flaskeh]*
brandy en cognac
bread brød *[bruh]*
coffee kaffe *[kafeh]*
cup en kopp *[ayn kop]*
dry tørr *[tur]*
fork en gaffel *[ayn gafel]*
fruit juice fruksaft *[frewktsaft]*
glass et glass *[ayt glas]*
gin and tonic en gin og tonic *[ayn gin oh tonik]*
half-bottle en halv flaske *[ayn hal flaskeh]*
hot chocolate varm sjokolade *[varm shokolahdeh]*
ice is *[ees]*
knife en kniv *[ayn k-neev]*
lager en pils *[ayn peels]*
lemonade en sitronbrus *[ayn sitronbrewss]*
milk melk *[mehlk]*
mineral water mineralvann *[minerahlvan]*
mineral water (fizzy) Farris *(brand name)*
napkin en serviett
orange juice appelsinjuice *[apelseenjoos]*
pepper pepper
red wine rødvin *[ruhveen]*
rosé rosé *[roosay]*
salt salt
spoon en skje *[ayn sheh]*
sugar sukker *[sokker]*
sweet søt *[suht]*
tea te *[teh]*
water vann
whisky en whisky
white wine hvitvin *[veetveen]*

UNDERSTANDING THE MENU

agurk(er) 1. gherkins; 2. cucumber
akevitt aquavit *(spirit made from potatoes)*
alkoholfritt øl alcohol-free beer
and duck
ansjos anchovies
appelsin orange
appelsinbrus orangeade
aprikos apricot
asparges asparagus
bakt baked
banan banana
bankekjøtt brown meat and onion stew
barnemeny children's menu
barneporsjon children's portion
bernaisesaus béarnaise sauce — a rich sauce
　made from butter, egg yolks and spices
biff med løk fried steak with onions
bjørnebær blackberries
blomkål cauliflower
blåskjell mussels
bløtkake cream gâteau
bløtkokt egg soft-boiled egg
boller 1. buns; 2. dumplings; 3. balls made
　from fish or meat
bringebær raspberries
brun lapskaus beef and potato stew with rich
　brown gravy
brus sweet fizzy drinks
bryst breast
brød bread
buljong clear soup
butterdeig pastry
bønner beans
dagens middag dinner of the day
dagens rett dish of the day
dagens suppe soup of the day
dampet/dampkokt steamed
diverse various, sundry

drikkevarer drinks
druer grapes
dyrestek med viltsaus roast reindeer with
  game sauce made with cream
eddik vinegar
eggedosis egg nog
eggekrem thick custard
eggerøre cold scrambled eggs with chives
eksportøl strong lager
elg elk
eple apple
Farris fizzy mineral water *(brand name)*
fenalår cured leg of lamb
fersk suppe og kjøtt meal of vegetable broth
  as a starter, and boiled beef with potatoes and
  sweet & sour onion sauce as a main course
fersken peach
fisk fish
fiskeboller i hvit saus fish balls in white
  sauce
fiskegrateng fish soufflé
fiskepudding med rekesaus fish loaf with
  prawn sauce
fiskestuing i terteskjell fish and shellfish in
  white sauce served in puff pastry shells
flambert flambéed
flattbrød unleavened bread
fleskepannekake ham omelette
flyndre sole
fløte cream
fløterand med frukt cream and vanilla
  mousse with fruit
fløtesaus cream sauce
formiddagsmat snack lunch
forrett first course
franskbrød white bread with poppy seeds
franske poteter French potato flakes
frityrstekt deep-fried
frokost breakfast
frokostblanding breakfast cereal

frukt fruit
fylt stuffed
får mutton
fårikål traditional lamb and cabbage stew with whole peppers
garnert garnished
geitost sweet, brown Norwegian goat's cheese
gelé jelly *(sweet or savoury)*
glassert glazed
gravlaks cured salmon
gressløk chives
grillretter grilled dishes
grillstekt grilled
gryte/gryterett casserole
grønne bønner French beans
grønne erter peas
grønnsaker vegetables
grøt 1. porridge; 2. porridge-type dessert made from flour, oats or rice; 3. dessert made from boiled fruit, fruit juice and cornflour
gulrøtter carrots
gås goose
hakket chopped
halvtørr medium dry
hamburgerrygg smoked pork loin
hasselnøtter hazelnuts
havregrøt oatmeal porridge
hellefisk halibut
helstekt fried or roasted whole
hetvin fortified wine
hjemmelaget home-made
hoffdessert 'court dessert' — pyramid of meringues with chocolate, whipped cream and flaked almonds
hollandaisesaus hollandaise sauce made with butter and egg yolk *(served with poached fish)*
honning honey
hovedrett main course
hummer lobster
husets of the house

hveteboller buns
hvitløk garlic
hvitting whiting
hvitvin white wine
hårdkokt egg hard-boiled egg
høns(e) chicken
irsk kaffe Irish coffee
is ice cream
iskake ice cream cake
jordbær strawberries
juice fruit juice
kabaret in aspic
kaffe coffee
kaker cakes
kaldrøkt makrell cold smoked mackerel
kalkun turkey
kalv veal
kanel cinnamon
kantareller chanterelles *(yellow mushrooms)*
karaffel carafe of wine
karamellpudding med krem caramel
   custard with whipped cream
karbonade minced beef steak
karve caraway seeds
kirsebær cherries
kjeks biscuits
kjøtt meat
kjøttboller i brun saus meat balls in brown
   sauce
kjøttkaker minced beef balls in a brown sauce
kjøttpudding meat loaf
kneipbrød wheaten bread
knekkebrød crispbread
koldtbord cold buffet table
konfekt filled chocolates
kotelett chop
krabbe crab
kransekake 'wreath cake' — a tower of
   almond rings decorated with flags and
   crackers
krem whipped cream

kreps crayfish
kringle wreath baked with yeast and filled with almond paste, apples or raisins
krokanis vanilla ice cream with chopped toasted almonds and caramel
kryddersild cured, spiced raw herring
kylling chicken
kål cabbage
kålrot turnip
kålrulletter cabbage parcels of finely minced meat in sauce
lagerøl low alcohol lager
laks salmon
lam(me) lamb
lapskaus med grønnsaker boiled beef and potato stew with vegetables
lettøl low alcohol beer
leverpostei liver pâté
loff white bread
lumpe thin potato scone eaten with hot dogs
lunsj lunch
lutefisk cod soaked in lye served with white sauce and melted butter
lår leg
løk onion
makrell mackerel
mandel almond
marinert marinated
medisterkaker fried minced pork balls
medisterpølse fried or boiled pork sausage
meny menu
middag dinner
mineralvann 1. fizzy drinks; 2. mineral water
multe(r) cloudberries *(wild orange berries)*
napoleonskake 'Napoleon's cake' — puff pastry and custard sandwich
nypesuppe rosehip soup *(dessert)*
nyrer kidneys
oksehale oxtail
oksekarbonader lean minced beef steaks

oksestek roast beef
ost cheese
panert coated with breadcrumbs
pannekaker pancakes
pepperrot horseradish
persille parsley
pinnekjøtt salted, dried flank of lamb, boiled
  and served with mashed turnip
platte cold buffet tray
poteter potatoes
potetpuré mashed potatoes
purre leek
pålegg sandwich spread or cold meat for
  sandwiches
pære pear
pølser sausages *(usually smoked frankfurters)*
rabarbra rhubarb
rakørret marinated cured trout
reddiker radishes
reinsdyrstek roast reindeer
rekecocktail prawn cocktail
reker prawns
remuladesaus mayonnaise and whipped
  cream with chopped gherkins
rett dish, course
reven/revet/revne grated
ribbe og surkål roast flank of pork with sweet
  and sour cabbage flavoured with caraway
rips redcurrants
ris rice
riskrem cold rice pudding mixed with whipped
  cream and served with red sauce
ristet 1. toasted; 2. fried; 3. roast
roastbiff med løk rare roast fillet of beef with
  fried onions
rogn roe
rosenkål Brussels sprouts
rosiner raisins
rugbrød rye bread
rundstykke crusty roll

rype(r) grouse
rå raw
rød red
rødbeter beetroot
rødgrøt soft red berry 'jelly'
rødspette plaice
rødvin red wine
røket smoked
rømme soured cream
rømmegrøt soured cream and white flour
  porridge served with cinnamon and sugar
saft 1. juice; 2. squash
salat 1. lettuce; 2. salad
sei coalfish *(similar to cod)*
sennep mustard
service inkludert service charge included
sild herring
sitron lemon
sitronfromasj lemon mousse
sjampinjong field mushrooms
sjokoladepudding chocolate blancmange
sjokoladesaus chocolate sauce
skalldyr shellfish
skinke ham
sky meat juices
slangeagurk cucumber
smør butter
smørbrød open sandwich
snitter open sandwiches
solbær blackcurrants
Solo orangeade *(brand name)*
speilegg fried egg
spekemat tray with various kinds of cured,
  cold meat served with 'flattbrød'
spekesild cured, raw herring
spekeskinke cured leg of ham
spisekart menu
stangselleri celery
stek roast
stekt fried

stuing in cream or white sauce
sukkererter mange-tout
suppe soup
surkål sweet and sour cabbage with caraway
svin(e) pork
svinekam loin of pork
svisker prunes
syltetøy jam
søt sweet
tartarsaus mayonnaise with chopped egg,
   onion, capers and gherkins
tartarsmørbrød open sandwich with raw beef
   and raw yolk of egg, garnished with chopped
   onion and beetroot
tebriks puff pastry rolls with poppy seeds
tilslørte bondepiker 'farm maids with veil' —
   stewed apples with toasted breadcrumbs and
   whipped cream
torsk cod
tyttebær cowberries *(like cranberries)*
tørr dry
vafler waffles
vaniljeis vanilla ice cream
vaniljesaus custard sauce
vannbakkels choux pastry cakes with cream
varm sjokolade med krem hot chocolate
   with whipped cream
varm retter hot dishes
vegetarretter vegetarian dishes
vilt game
vinkart wine list
wienerbrød Danish pastry
wienerschnitzel fillet of veal fried in
   breadcrumbs
ål eel
øl beer
ørret trout
østers oysters

Iɴ Portugal, you will find a wide variety of excellent eating places which cater for every taste and pocket. **Restaurantes** serve meals between 12 p.m. and 3 p.m. and from 7 p.m. to 10 p.m. In between these times, you can go to any **café** or **pastelaria** where you will be able to choose from a large range of pastries, cakes and sandwiches. However, if you need something a bit more substantial, then a **snack-bar** or **cervejaria** is the place to go. These are bar-restaurants where you can have a light meal like a **prego** (steak sandwich) or a **combinado** (hamburgers, omelettes, chips, eggs, salads etc.) at any time of the day, although some places may serve only full meals at lunch and dinner time. After ten at night there are still some places open, mainly in the big cities, which will serve light meals and snacks till about one in the morning.

All restaurants have **pratos do dia** (today's specials) which are cheaper and served more quickly than other items. Some restaurants may also have **refeição turística**, a set menu which is very reasonably priced and well worth a try. Portions are usually generous and the menu tends to vary slightly from region to region.

Alcohol is available in all of the above establishments at any time of the day. Portuguese wine is good and is excellent value. The most well-known wine is **vinho verde**, a slightly sparkling wine made from young grapes. If you like an after-dinner drink, try a **Carvalho Ribeiro e Ferreira** brandy or **Aguadente de Medronho**.

Service charge is normally included in the price, but it is customary to leave a tip.

ORDERING

excuse me!
se faz favor!
[suh fash fuh-vor]

can I order please?
posso mandar vir?
[possoo mandahr veer]

one . . ./two . . .
um (uma) . . ./dois (duas) . . .
[oom (oomuh)/doysh (dooash)]

that's for me/him
isso é para mim/para ele
[eessoo eh paruh meeng/paruh ehl]

can I see the menu again?
posso ver a lista outra vez?
[possoo vehr uh leeshtuh ohtruh vez]

can you bring another red wine/beer?
pode-me trazer mais vinho tinto/cerveja?
[pod-muh trazair mysh veenyoo teengtoo/serveh-juh]

could I have the bill please?
pode-me trazer a conta, por favor?
[pod-muh trazair uh kontuh poor fuh-vor]

if the waiter/waitress says:
  a comida estava boa?
  [uh koomeedah stah-vuh boh-uh]
  did you enjoy your meal?

you could reply:
  estava muito boa, obrigado
  [stah-vuh mweentuh boh-uh obreegah-doo]
  it was very nice, thank you

SOME BASIC WORDS

beer uma cerveja *[ooma serveh-juh]*
bottle uma garrafa *[ooma garrah-fuh]*
brandy um brandy *[oom bran-dee]*
bread pão *[powng]*
coffee um café *[oom kuffeh]*
cup uma chávena *[ooma shavvenuh]*
dry seco *[seh-koo]*
fork um garfo *[oom garfoo]*
fruit juice um sumo de fruta *[oom soomo duh froo-tuh]*
glass um copo *[oom kopoo]*
gin and tonic um gin tónico *[oom geeng tonee-koo]*
half-bottle uma meia-garrafa *[ooma may-yuh-garrah-fuh]*
hot chocolate um chocolate quente *[oom shoo-koo-lat kent]*
ice gelo *[jeloo]*
knife uma faca *[ooma fah-kah]*
lager uma cerveja *[ooma serveh-juh]*
lemonade uma limonada *[ooma leemoo-na-duh]*
milk leite *[layt]*
mineral water água mineral *[ahg-wuh mee-nuhral]*
mineral water (fizzy) água com gás *[ahg-wuh kong gash]*
napkin um guardanapo *[oom gwarduh-napoo]*
orange juice um sumo de laranja *[oom soomoo duh luh-rang-juh]*
pepper pimenta *[peementuh]*
red wine vinho tinto *[veenyoo teengtoo]*
rosé rosé *[rozay]*
salt sal
spoon uma colher *[ooma kool-yair]*
sugar açúcar *[assookar]*
sweet doce *[dos]*
tea um chá *[oom sha]*

water água *[ahg-wuh]*
whisky um whisky *[oom weeskee]*
white wine vinho branco *[veenyoo brang-koo]*

UNDERSTANDING THE MENU

açorda de alho thick bread soup with garlic
  and herbs
açorda de marisco thick bread soup with
  shellfish
aguardente brandy
aguardentes bagaceiras grape brandies
aguardentes velhas e preparadas matured
  brandies
Aldeia Velha very strong clear spirit
alface lettuce
alheira garlic sausage
almoço lunch
almôndegas meat balls
amêijoas clams
amêijoas à Bulhão Pato clams with onion,
  coriander and garlic
amêijoas na cataplana clams in a sweet
  tomato sauce served in a large dish
amêndoa amarga bitter almond liqueur
ananás pineapple
anho à moda do Minho roast lamb and roast
  potatoes
arroz à valenciana rice served with chicken,
  pork and sea food
arroz branco rice
arroz de frango fried chicken in wine, ham
  and rice casserole
arroz de marisco rice with shell fish
arroz doce rice dessert
atum tuna
azeitonas olives
azeitonas recheadas stuffed olives
bacalhau à brás cod with egg and fried
  potatoes

bacalhau à Gomes de Sá cod baked with parsley, potatoes, onions and olives
bacalhau assado grilled cod.
bacalhau à Zé do Pipo cod in an egg sauce
bacalhau com natas cod with cream
bacalhau dourado baked cod
bacalhau grelhado grilled cod
bacalhau nas brasas barbecued cod
batata assada baked potato
batatas potatoes
batatas cozidas boiled potatoes
batatas fritas chips
bavaroise egg whites and cream dessert
bebida drink
berbigão mussel-like shell fish
beringelas aubergines
bica small black coffee *(like espresso)*
bifanas pork slice in a roll
bife steak
bife à cortador thick tender steak
bife de alcatra rump steak
bife de vaca (com ovo a cavalo) steak (with an egg on top)
bife grelhado grilled steak
bife tártaro steak tartare
bifes de cebolada steak with onions
bifinhos de porco small slices of pork
bifinhos nas brasas small slices of barbecued beef
bolachas biscuits
bola de carne meat ball
bolo de chocolate chocolate cake
bolo de nozes walnut cake
bolo inglês sponge cake with dried fruit
bolos cakes
borrego lamb
brioche round bun
cachorros hot dogs
café coffee
café com leite white coffee

café duplo double espresso coffee
caldeirada mixed fish with onions and
potatoes
caldo de carne meat soup
caldo verde potato broth with shredded
cabbage
camarões prawns
canja de galinha chicken soup
capilé drink make with water, sugar and syrup
caracóis snails
caranguejos crabs
carapaus fritos fried mackerel
carapinhada de café coffee drink with
crushed ice
carapinhada de groselha blackcurrant drink
with crushed ice
caril curry
carioca small weak black coffee
carne de porco com amêijoas pork with
clams
carne de vaca assada roast beef
carne de vaca guisada stewed beef
carne estufada stewed meat
carnes meats
carnes frias selection of cold meats
cerveja beer or lager
cerveja branca lager
cerveja de pressão draught beer
cerveja preta bitter *(beer)*
chá tea
chá de limão lemon tea
chantilly whipped cream
charlotte biscuits with fruit and cream
chocolate glacé iced chocolate
chocolate quente hot chocolate
chouriço spiced sausage
cimbalino small black coffee
codorniz quail
codornizes fritas fried quail
coelho frito fried rabbit

coentros coriander
cogumelos mushrooms
conquilhas baby clams
corvina large sea fish
costeletas chops
costeletas de porco pork chops
costeletas fritas fried chops
costeletas grelhadas grilled chops
couve branca white cabbage
couve-flor cauliflower
couve-flor com molho branco no forno cauliflower cheese
couve roxa red cabbage
cozido à portuguesa a stew of boiled beef, gammon, smoked sausage, rice and vegetables
creme de cogumelos cream of mushroom soup
creme de marisco cream of shellfish soup
crepe de camarão prawn crêpe
crepe crêpe, pancake
doce 1. sweet *(wine)*; 2. jam; 3. sweet, dessert
doces de ovos egg custard dessert
éclair de chantilly whipped cream éclair
éclairs de café coffee éclairs
ementa menu
empadão de carne large meat pie
enguias fritas fried eels
ensopado de enguias eel stew
entradas starters
entrecosto com amêijoas entrecôte with clams
ervilhas peas
escalope escalope
escalope ao Madeira escalope with Madeira wine
escalope de porco pork escalope
escalope panado breaded escalope
espargos asparagus
esparguete à bolonhesa spaghetti bolognese
esparregado spinach purée

espetada mista mixed kebab
espinafres salteados spinach in butter sauce
faisão pheasant
farófias whipped egg white mixed with milk,
  egg custard, vanilla and cinammon
febras de porco thin slices of pork
feijoada stew made of pig's feet, sausage, white
  beans and cabbage
feijão verde French beans
foie gras goose or duck liver pâté
frango chicken
frango assado roast chicken
frango na púcara chicken stewed in Port and
  brandy, fried with almonds
frango no churrasco barbecued chicken
frango no espeto spit-roast chicken
fruta fruit
fruta da época seasonal fruit
galão large milky coffee
galinha de fricassé chicken fricassee
gambas prawns
gambas grelhadas grilled prawns
garoto small coffee with milk
gaspacho chilled soup made from green
  peppers, tomato and cucumber
gelado ice cream
gelado de baunilha vanilla ice cream
ginja cherry
ginginha cherry liqueur
groselha blackcurrant
guisado stew
hamburguer com batatas fritas hamburger
  and chips
hamburguer com ovo hamburger with an egg
hamburguer no pão hamburger roll
hortaliças green vegetables
italiana half an espresso coffee
jantar 1. dinner *(evening meal)*; 2. supper
jardineira vegetable stew
lagosta lobster

lagosta thermidor lobster thermidor
lagostins crayfish
lampreia à moda do Minho marinated
  lamprey in a thick sauce
lanche afternoon tea
laranjas oranges
lasanha lasagne
legumes vegetables
leitão da Bairrada sucking pig from Bairrada
leite milk
leite creme light custard flavoured with
  cinnamon
limonada 1. fresh lemon juice with water;
  2. lemonade
linguado à meunière sole meunière *(served in
  butter, lemon juice and herbs)*
linguado frito fried sole
linguado grelhado grilled sole
linguado no forno baked sole
lista de preços price list
lista dos vinhos wine list
lombo de porco loin of pork
lombo de vaca sirloin
lulas fritas fried squid
lulas guisadas stewed squid
lulas recheadas stuffed squid
maçã assada baked apple
maçãs apples
macedónia de frutas fruit cocktail
manteiga butter
manteiga queimada butter sauce used with
  fish
marisco shellfish
marmelada quince jam
mayonnaise mayonnaise
mayonnaise de alho garlic mayonnaise
mazagrin iced coffee with lemon
meia de leite large white coffee
meio seco medium dry
melancia watermelon

melão melon
melão com presunto melon with ham
merengue meringue
mexilhões mussels
mil folhas sweet flaky pastry
molho à Espanhola spicy onion and garlic sauce
molho béchamel white sauce
molho mornay white sauce with cheese
molho tártaro tartare sauce *(mayonnaise with herbs, gherkins and capers)*
morangos strawberries
morangos com chantilly strawberries and whipped cream
morangos com natas strawberries and cream
morena mixture of lager and bitter
mousse de chocolate chocolate mousse
mousse de leite condensado condensed milk mousse
omolette omelette
omolette de fiambre ham omelette
omolette de marisco shellfish omelette
omolette de presunto cured ham omelette
omolette de queijo cheese omelette
ovo estrelado fried egg
ovos à Minhota baked eggs, tomatoes and onions
ovos mexidos scrambled eggs
ovos mexidos com tomate scrambled eggs and tomatoes
ovos verdes stuffed eggs
pão de centeio rye bread
pão de milho corn bread
pão torrado toasted bread
pargo sea-bream
pargo assado roast bream
pargo cozido boiled bream
parrilhada grilled fish
pastel 1. cake; 2. pie
pastelinhos de bacalhau fish cakes made with cod

paté de fígado liver pâté
pato assado roast duck
pato com laranja duck à l'orange
peixe fish
peixe espada swordfish
pequeno almoço breakfast
pequeno almoço continental continental breakfast
pequeno almoço inglês English-style breakfast
pêra abacate avocado pear
pêra bela Helena pear in chocolate sauce
pêras pears
percebes type of shellfish
perdizes de escabeche marinated partridge
perdizes fritas fried partridge
perdizes na púcara partridge casserole
perna de carneiro assada roast leg of lamb
perú turkey
perú assado roast turkey
pescada cozida boiled hake
pescadinhas de rabo na boca haddock served with their tails in their mouths
pêssegos peaches
petit-fours small cakes
pimentos red or green peppers
prato do dia today's special
prato especial da casa speciality of the house
pratos combinados mixed dishes
prego thin slice of steak in a roll
presunto cured ham
pudim de ovos egg pudding
pudim flã crème caramel
pudim molotov crème caramel with egg white
puré de batata mashed potatoes
pv (preço variado) price varies
queijo da Ilha strong peppery cheese from Madeira
queijo da Serra cheese from the Serra da Estrela

queijo de Azeitão cheese matured in olive oil
queijo de Elvas mild white cheese
queijo fresco very mild goat's milk cheese
queijos cheeses
refeição ligeira snack
rins kidneys
rins ao Madeira kidney served with Madeira
  wine
rissol de camarão prawn rissole
rolo de carne meat roll or loaf
salada de agriões cress salad
salada de atum tuna salad
salada de frutas fruit salad
salada de lagosta lobster salad
salada mista mixed salad
salada russa salad of diced vegetables in
  mayonnaise
salmão salmon
salmão fumado smoked salmon
salmonetes grelhados grilled mullet
salsicha sausage
salsichas de porco pork sausages
sandes de fiambre ham sandwich
sandes de lombo steak sandwich
sandes de paio sausage sandwich
sandes de presunto ham sandwich
sandes mista mixed sandwich
santola spider crab
santola gratinada spider crab au gratin
sapateira spider crab
sardinhas assadas charcoal-grilled sardines
seco dry
selecção de queijos selection of cheeses
sobremesas desserts
solha assada no forno baked flounder
solha frita fried flounder
sopa de agriões cress soup
sopa de camarão prawn soup
sopa de cebola gratinada onion soup au
  gratin

sopa de pão e coentros bread and coriander
  soup
sopa de pedra thick vegetable soup
sopa dourada dessert made from eggs
sopa juliana vegetable soup
sopas soups
soufflé de camarão prawn soufflé
sumo de laranja orange juice
sumo de maçã apple juice
tarte de amêndoa almond tart
tarte de maçã apple tart
tinto red
toranja grapefruit
tortilha Spanish omelette with potato
tosta toasted sandwich
tosta mista ham and cheese toasted sandwich
truta trout
uvas brancas/pretas white/black grapes
vinho branco white wine
vinho de mesa table wine
vinho do Porto Port wine
vinho espumante sparkling wine
vinho tinto red wine
vinho verde slightly sparkling wine made from
  unripe grapes

SPANISH food varies greatly from region to region. For example, in the north-west you will find that fish is usually grilled or steamed, while in the Basque country, it is cooked in a sauce made with wine and peppers or parsley. It is true that you can find famous dishes like **paella** all over Spain, but each area has its own special way of preparing it. Spanish food is generally very simple, with an emphasis on fresh ingredients. Olive oil is normally used in cooking rather than butter.

Meal times differ, depending on the region, but are usually later than you would expect in the UK. Although breakfast tends to be a very light meal, lunch can be as late as 3 o'clock. Evening meals are also served very late. Many Spaniards prefer to eat as late as 10 p.m. and traditional restaurants are unlikely to open until about 8.30 p.m. However, in tourist areas, meals may be served earlier than this. In between, you can go to some of the many bars and sample the **tapas**, which are snacks that you can have with your wine. (You can order larger portions of **tapas** separately.)

The best known wine is **Rioja**, but it's worth trying local wines, and of course you can always get **sangria** a mixture of red wine and orange juice with pieces of orange and lemon.

ORDERING

waiter/waitress!
¡camarero/señorita por favor!
[kamare*hro*/sehnyore*e*ta por fab*o*r]

excuse me!
¡por favor!
[por fab*o*r]

can I order please?
quisiera pedir, por favor
[keessee-ehra peh-deer por fabor]

one glass/a bottle/two . . .
un vaso/una botella/dos . . .
[oon basso/oona botehya]

that's for me/him
eso es para mí/él
[ehsso ess para mee/ehl]

can I see the menu again?
¿podría ver la carta otra vez?
[podree-a ber la karta ohtra beth]

**can you bring me another red wine/
mineral water?**
¿podría traerme otra botella de vino tinto/agua
mineral?
[podree-a tra-ermeh ohtra botehya deh beeno
teento/agwah meeneral]

some more bread please
un poco más de pan por favor
[oon poko mass deh pan por fabor]

could I have the bill please?
la cuenta, por favor
[la kwenta por fabor]

if the waiter/waitress says:
¿le gustó la comida?
[leh goosto la kommeeda]
did you enjoy your meal?

you could say:
sí, muchas gracias
[see moochass grathyass]
yes, thank you

SOME BASIC WORDS

beer una cerveza *[oona thairbeh-tha]*
bottle una botella *[oona botehya]*
brandy un brandy
bread pan
coffee un café *[oon kafeh]*
cup una taza *[oona tatha]*
dry seco *[seko]*
fork un tenedor *[oon tenehdor]*
fruit juice un zumo de fruta *[oon thoomo deh froota]*
glass un vaso *[oon basso]*
gin and tonic una ginebra con tónica *[oona Heenehbra kon toneeka]*
half-bottle una media botella *[oona meh-dya botehya]*
hot chocolate una taza de chocolate *[oona tatha deh chokola-teh]*
ice hielo *[yehlo]*
knife un cuchillo *[oon koochee-yo]*
lager una cerveza *[oona thairbeh-tha]*
lemonade una limonada *[oona leemonahda]*
milk leche *[leh-cheh]*
mineral water agua mineral *[agwah meeneral]*
mineral water (fizzy) agua mineral con gas *[agwah meeneral kon gass]*
napkin una servilleta *[oona serbeeyeh-ta]*
orange juice un zumo de naranja *[oon thoomo deh naranHa]*
pepper pimienta *[peemyen-ta]*
red wine vino tinto *[beeno teento]*
rosé rosado *[rosahdo]*
salt sal
spoon una cuchara *[oona koochara]*
sugar azúcar *[athookar]*
sweet dulce *[dooltheh]*
tea un té *[oon teh]*
water agua *[agwah]*
whisky un whisky *[oon weeskee]*
white wine vino blanco *[beeno blanko]*

UNDERSTANDING THE MENU

aceitunas olives
aguacate avocado
ahumados variados smoked fish
ajo garlic
albóndigas meat balls
alcachofas con jamón artichokes with ham
alcachofas salteadas sautéed artichokes
alcaparras capers
almejas a la buena mujer clams stewed with chillis, wine, lemon and herbs
almejas a la marinera clams stewed in wine and parsley
almejas naturales live clams
alubias con . . . beans with . . .
ancas de rana frog's legs
anchoas anchovies
angulas baby eels
apio celery
arenque herring
arroz a la cubana boiled rice with fried eggs and bananas
arroz con leche rice pudding
asados de . . . roast . . .
atún al horno baked tuna
bacalao al pil pil cod with chillis and garlic
batido de chocolate chocolate milkshake
bebidas drinks
berenjenas a la crema aubergines in cream sauce
besugo al horno baked sea bream
bistec de ternera veal steak
bizcochos sponge fingers
bomba helada baked alaska
bonito al horno baked tuna
boquerones fritos fried fresh anchovies
brazo de gitano sort of swiss roll
butifarra Catalan sausage
cabrito asado roast kid

....

cachelada pork stew with eggs, tomato and
  onion
café con leche white coffee
calamares a la romana squid rings fried in a
  batter
calamares en su tinta squid cooked in their
  ink
calamares fritos fried squid
caldereta gallega vegetable stew
caldo de pescado clear fish soup
caldo gallego clear soup with green vegetables,
  beans and pork
caldo guanche soup made with potatoes,
  onions, tomatoes and courgettes
callos a la madrileña tripe cooked with chillis
camarones baby prawns
caña small beer
cangrejos de río river crabs
caracoles snails
carbonada de buey beef cooked in beer
carnes meats
carro de queso cheese board
cena dinner *(evening meal)*
centollo spider crab
cesta de frutas assortment of fresh fruit
champiñones a la crema mushrooms with
  cream sauce
chanfaina rice and black pudding stew
chanquetes fish *(like whitebait)*
chipirones squid
chuleta de buey beef chop
chuleta de cerdo pork chop
chuletas de cordero (con ali oli) lamb
  chops (with garlic mayonnaise)
chuletitas de cordero small lamb chops
chuletón large chop
chuletón de buey large beef chop
churros fried pastry cut into lengths
cigalas a la parrilla grilled crayfish
cochinillo asado roast sucking pig

cocido castellano o madrileño stew made
 with meat, chickpeas and vegetables
cocochas (de merluza) hake stew
cóctel de gambas prawn cocktail
cóctel de langostinos king prawn cocktail
cóctel de mariscos seafood cocktail
codornices asadas roast quail
coles de bruselas salteadas sautéed
 Brussels sprouts
coliflor cauliflower
comida 1. lunch; 2. meal
conejo asado roast rabbit
conejo estofado stewed rabbit
consomé al jerez consommé with sherry
cordero asado roast lamb
cordero chilindrón lamb stew with onion,
 peppers and tomatoes
costillas de cerdo con chucrut pork ribs
 with sauerkraut
crema catalana crème brûlée
crema de espárragos cream of asparagus
 soup
criadillas bull's testicles
criadillas (de tierra) truffles *(edible fungus
 found underground)*
crocante ice cream with chopped nuts
croquetas de huevo egg croquettes
cuajada junket
desayuno breakfast
embutidos variados assorted sausages
empanada gallega pie with chicken, chorizo,
 peppers and ham
empanadillas de bonito small tuna pies
empanadillas de chorizo spiced sausage pies
ensaimada mallorquina cake
ensalada de pollo chicken salad
ensalada mixta mixed salad
ensalada simple green salad
ensaladilla (rusa) Russian salad
entrecot a la parrilla grilled entrecôte

....

entremeses de la casa hors d'oeuvres
entremeses variados hors d'oeuvres
escalope a la milanesa breaded veal with cheese
escalope de lomo de cerdo escalope of fillet of pork
escalope de ternera escalope of veal
espadín a la toledana kebab
espárragos asparagus
espinacas a la crema spinach à la crème
estofado de . . . . . . stew
fabada (asturiana) bean stew with sausage
faisán estofado stewed pheasant
filete a la parrilla grilled veal steak
filete de cerdo pork steak
filete de ternera veal steak
flan crème caramel
fresas con nata strawberries with cream
fruta variada fruit
gallina em pepitoria stewed chicken with peppers
gambas al ajillo prawns with garlic
gambas a la plancha grilled prawns
gambas con mayonesa prawns with mayonnaise
gambas rebozadas prawns in batter
garbanzos chickpeas
gazpacho andaluz cold soup made with tomatoes, onions, cucumber and garlic
gazpacho manchego rabbit stew with tomato and garlic *(sometimes also with partridge meat)*
gelatina de . . . . . . jelly
guisantes salteados con jamón sautéed peas with ham
helado de caramelo caramel ice cream
helado de fresa strawberry ice cream
helado de mantecado vanilla ice cream
helado de nata vanilla ice cream
helado de vainilla vanilla ice cream
hígado encebollado liver in an onion sauce

hígado estofado braised liver
higos con miel y nueces figs with honey and
   nuts
horchata (de chufas) almond-flavoured milk
   drink
huevos eggs
huevos a la flamenca baked eggs with
   sausage, tomato, peas, asparagus and peppers
huevos con jamón eggs with ham
huevos escalfados poached eggs
huevos fritos con chorizo fried eggs with
   Spanish sausage
huevos pasados por agua boiled eggs
huevos rellenos stuffed eggs
huevos revueltos con tomate scrambled
   eggs with tomato
jamón (serrano) cured ham
jarra de vino wine jug
jerez amontillado pale dry sherry
jerez fino pale light sherry
jerez oloroso sweet sherry
jeta pig's cheeks
judias verdes green beans
jugo de naranja orange juice
jugo de melocotón peach juice
jugo de piña apple juice
jugo de tomate tomato juice
lacón con grelos bacon with turnip tops
langosta a la americana lobster with brandy
   and garlic
langosta con mahonesa lobster with
   mayonnaise
langostinos a la plancha grilled king prawns
leche frita slices of thick custard fried in
   breadcrumbs
lengua (de buey) (ox) tongue
lengua de cordero estofada stewed lamb
   tongue
lenguado a la plancha grilled sole
lenguado a la romana sole in batter

lenguado menie/meuniere sole meunière
lentejas aliñadas lentils with vinaigrette
licores 1. alcohol; 2. liqueurs
liebre estofada stewed hare
lubina al horno baked sea bass
macedonia de frutas fruit salad
manises peanuts
manos de cerdo pig's trotters
mantecadas small cakes
mantequilla butter
manzanas asadas baked apples
manzanilla dry sherry-type wine
mariscada cold mixed shellfish
mariscos del día fresh shellfish
mazápan marzipan
mejillones mussels
melocotones en almibar peaches in syrup
melón con jamón melon with cured ham
menestra de verduras vegetable stew
menú de la casa fixed price menu
menú del día set menu
merienda tea *(afternoon snack)*
merluza a la plancha grilled hake
merluza a la vasca hake in a garlic sauce
merluza frita fried hake
mermelada de fresa strawberry jam
mermelada de naranja orange jam
mero a la parrilla grilled grouper *(fish)*
mollejas de ternera fritas fried sweetbreads
morcilla black pudding
natillas cold custard with cinnamon
orejas y pie de cerdo pig's ears and trotters
otros mariscos según precios en
  plaza other shellfish, depending on current
  prices
paella castellana fried rice with meat
paella de marisco fried rice with shellfish
paella de pollo chicken paella
paella valenciana fried rice with various
  shellfish and chicken

pan bread
panaché de verduras vegetable stew
panceta bacon
parrillada de mariscos mixed grilled
   shellfish
pastel de ... 1. ... cake; 2. ... pie
patatas asadas roast potatoes
patatas bravas potatoes in cayenne sauce
patatas fritas 1. chips; 2. crisps
pato a la naranja duck à l'orange
pavipollo large chicken
pavo asado roast duck
pavo relleno stuffed turkey
pechuga de pollo breast of chicken
peixo-palo a la marinera stock-fish with
   potatoes and tomatoes
pepinillos gherkins
pepino cucumber
percebes shell fish *(edible barnacles)*
perdices asadas roast partridges
perdices con chocolate partridges with
   chocolate
pescaditos fritos fried sprats
pichones estofados stewed pigeon
pimientos morrones strong peppers
pimientos rellenos stuffed peppers
piña fresca fresh pineapple
pinchos morunos kebabs
pisto fried peppers, onions, tomatoes and
   courgettes
plátanos bananas
platos combinados mixture of various foods
   served as one dish (e.g. meat, chips and
   vegetables)
pollo al ajillo fried chicken with garlic
pollo asado roast chicken
pollo en pepitoria chicken in wine with
   saffron, garlic and almonds
pollos tomateros con zanhorias young
   chicken with carrots

pulpitos con cebolla baby octopuses with onions
pulpo octopus
purrusalda cod with leeks and potatoes
queso del país local cheese
queso manchego hard, strong cheese from La Mancha
quisquillas shrimps
ración de . . . portion of . . .
ragout de ternera veal ragoût
rape a la plancha grilled white fish
remolacha beetroot
repostería de la casa cakes and desserts made on the premises
requesón cream cheese
revuelto de ajos tiernos scrambled egg with spring garlic
revuelto de angulas scrambled egg with baby eels
revuelto de gambas scrambled egg with prawns
revuelto de sesos scrambled egg with brains
revuelto de trigueros scrambled egg with asparagus
riñones kidneys
riñones al jerez kidneys in a sherry sauce
rodaballo turbot
romesco de pescado mixed fish
rovellons mushrooms *(Catalonian)*
salchichas sausages
salchichas de Frankfurt frankfurters
salchichón salami-type sausage
salmón ahumado smoked salmon
salmón a la parrilla grilled salmon
salmonetes red mullet
salpicón de mariscos shellfish with vinaigrette
salsa allioli garlic mayonnaise
salsa mayonesa mayonnaise
salsa vinagreta sauce vinaigrette

sangría mixture of red wine, lemonade, spirits and fruit

sardinas a la brasa barbecued sardines

sardinas a la parrilla grilled sardines

seco dry

semidulce medium sweet

sesos a la romana fried brains in batter

setas a la plancha grilled mushrooms

shangurro (centollo relleno) spider crab cooked in its shell

solomillo con patatas fritas fillet steak with chips

solomillo de ternera fillet of veal

solomillo de vaca fillet of beef

sopa de ajo bread and garlic soup

sopa de fideos noodle soup

sopa de gallina chicken soup

sopa de marisco fish and shellfish soup

sopa de pescado fish soup

sopa del día soup of the day

sopa de verduras vegetable soup

soufflé de queso cheese soufflé

suplemento de verduras extra vegetables

tallarines tagliatelle

tarta de chocolate chocolate gâteau

tarta de la casa tart baked on the premises

tarta de manzana apple tart

tarta helada ice-cream gâteau

tarta moca mocha tart

té tea

tencas tench *(fish)*

ternera asada roast veal

tocinillo de cielo rich, thick crème caramel

tortilla a su gusto omelette made to the customer's wishes

tortilla de champiñones mushroom omelette

tortilla de espárragos asparagus omelette

tortilla de patatas potato omelette

tortilla de setas mushroom omelette

tortilla española potato omelette

tortilla francesa plain omelette
tostón asado roast sucking pig
tournedó tournedos *(fillet steak)*
trucha ahumada smoked trout
trucha escabechada marinated trout
truchas con jamón trout with ham
trufas truffles *(edible fungus)*
turbante de arroz rice served with steak,
    sausage, peppers and bacon
turrón nougat *(eaten at Christmas)*
vaca estofada stewed beef
vino blanco white wine
vino de la casa house wine
vino rosado rosé wine
vino tinto red wine
vieiras scallops
zarzuela de mariscos seafood stew
zarzuela de pescados y mariscos fish and
    shellfish stew
zumo de limón lemon juice
zumo de naranja orange juice

Eating places in Sweden range from top-class restaurants to simple cafés serving inexpensive meals. There is a wide choice of middle-of-the-range restaurants for the tourist on a limited budget. You will often see a sign for **Dagens rätt**, the special dish of the day, often reasonably priced, and this usually includes a salad, a soft drink and coffee. The traditional Swedish **smörgåsbord** should not be missed. This is a cold buffet consisting of herring and other fish, assorted meats and salads, where you can eat as much as you like for a set price.

Lunch is generally served from the unusually early time of 11.30 a.m. and dinner can be as early as 5 p.m. However, mealtimes are flexible and many restaurants serve meals throughout the afternoon. The service charge is always included in the bill but you may leave an additional tip if you wish.

In Sweden, beer is the most popular alcoholic drink and there are four types: **lättöl** *[letturl]* which is fairly weak, **folköl** *[follkurl]* and **mellanöl** *[mellanurl]* which are medium strength and **starköl** *[starkurl]* which is strong.

ORDERING

waiter!/waitress!
hovmästarn!/fröken!
[hawvmestahrn/frurken]

excuse me!
ursäkta
[ewrsekta]

can I order please?
kan jag få beställa
[kan yah faw bestella]

one .../two ...
en .../två ...
[ayn .../tvaw ...]

that's for me/him
det här är för mig/honom
[dey hair ay furr may/honom]

can I see the menu again?
kan jag få se matsedeln en gång till
[kan yah faw say mahtsaydeln ayn gawng till]

can you bring me another red wine/beer?
kan jag få ett glas rödvin till/en öl till
[kan yah faw ett glass rurveen till/en url till]

could I have the bill please?
kan jag få notan
[kan jah faw nootan]

if the waiter/waitress says
  var det gott?
  [vahr day gott]
  did you enjoy your meal?

you could reply
  ja, tack
  [yah tack]
  yes, thank you

SOME BASIC WORDS

beer en öl *[ayn url]*
bottle en flaska *[ayn flaska]*
brandy en konjak *[ayn konyahk]*
bread ett bröd *[ett brurd]*
coffee kaffe *[kaffeh]*

cup en kopp *[ayn kopp]*
dry torr *[tor]*
fork en gaffel *[ayn gaffel]*
fruit juice en juice *[ayn yooss]*
glass ett glas *[ett glahss]*
gin and tonic en gin och tonic *[ayn gin ock tonnik]*
half-bottle en halv flaska *[ayn hahlv flaska]*
hot chocolate en (varm) choklad *[ayn (vahrm) shoklahd]*
ice is *[ees]*
knife en kniv *[ayn k-neev]*
lager en pilsner *[ayn peelsner]*
lemonade en läsk *[ayn lesk]*
milk mjölk
mineral water mineralvatten *[minerahlvatten]*
mineral water (fizzy) kolsyrat vatten *[kohlsewraht vatten]*
napkin en servett *[ayn sairvett]*
orange juice en apelsin juice *[ayn ahpelseen yooss]*
pepper peppar *[peppahr]*
red wine rödvin *[rurveen]*
rosé rosé *[rossay]*
salt salt *[sahlt]*
spoon en sked *[ayn shayd]*
sugar socker
sweet söt *[surt]*
tea te *[tee]*
water vatten
whisky en whisky *[ayn whisky]*
white wine vitt vin *[vitt veen]*

UNDERSTANDING THE MENU

abborre perch
aladåb fish or meat in aspic
akvavit schnapps *(potato-based liquor)*
and wild duck

anka duck
ansjovis anchovies
ansjovisfräs (gubbröra) fried anchovies with
hard-boiled eggs and onion
apelsin orange
apelsinris rice pudding with oranges
bakad potatis baked potatoes
bakelse cake, pastry, tart
barkis, bergis French loaf with poppy seeds
biff beef
biff à la Lindström burgers made of beef,
potato, egg, cream, beetroot and capers
biffgryta beef casserole
biff med lök beef with onions
biffpaj beef pie
biff Rydberg a hash of diced steak, potatoes
and onions
björnbär blackberry
blekselleri blanched celery
blodpudding black pudding
blomkål cauliflower
blomkålspuré cauliflower purée
blåbär blaeberry, bilberry
blåkokt forell trout poached in wine vinegar
bruna bönor baked brown beans
brylépudding caramel custard
brysselkål brussels sprouts
bräckt bacon quick-fried bacon
bräserad fiskfilé braised fillet of fish
bullar buns, rolls
bärkräm berry fool
bärpaj berry pie
böckling smoked Baltic herring
bönor beans
champinjonsoppa cream of mushroom soup
citronfromage lemon mousse
curryhöns chicken curry
druvor grapes
efterrätt dessert
falukorv fried pork sausage

fasan pheasant
fasangryta casserole of pheasant
fattiga riddare bread dipped in eggs and milk
and fried, served with jam and cream
fiskaladåb fish in aspic
fiskbullar fish balls
fiskbullsgryta casserole made with fish balls
fiskfilé fillet of fish
fiskfärs minced fish
fiskgratäng fish au gratin
fiskgryta fish casserole
fisksoppa fish soup
fisksufflé fish soufflé
flundra flounder
fläsk 1. pork; 2. bacon
fläskfilé fillet of pork
fläskfärsrulader roulades of minced pork
fläskkorv boiled spicy pork sausage
fläskkotlett pork chop
fläskpannkaka pancake filled with pork
fläskstek joint of pork
folköl medium strength beer
forell trout
fransk omelett French omelette
frikadeller forcemeat balls
friterad potatis chips
fruktkompott stewed fruit
fullkornsbröd wholemeal bread
fyllda stekta äpplen stuffed roast apples
förlorat ägg poached egg
glaserad skinka glazed ham
glasmästarsill salt herring marinated with
horseradish and carrot
glass ice cream
glass med maräng ice cream with meringue
grahamsbröd brown bread
gratinerad löksoppa onion soup au gratin
gravad strömming raw spiced herring
gravlax raw spiced salmon
griljerad skinka glazed ham

grillad korv grilled sausage
grillat revbensspjäll grilled spare-ribs
grön ärtpuré green pea purée
gröna ärter green peas
grönkål kale
grönsakssoppa vegetable soup
grönsallad lettuce
gul lök yellow onion
gurka cucumber
gädda pike
gädda med pepparrot pike with horseradish
hallon raspberry
helstekt entrecote whole roast entrecôte
helstekt oxfilé whole roast fillet of beef
hjortron cloudberry *(like cranberry)*
hovdessert (marängsviss) meringue layered
    with whipped cream and melted plain
    chocolate
hönsfrikassé chicken fricassee
hönsgryta chicken casserole
hönssoppa chicken soup
inbakad oxfilé fillet of beef baked in pastry
inkokt fisk cold boiled fish
inlagd rödbetor pickled beetroot
inlagd gurka pickled gherkins
inlagd sill marinated salt herring
Janssons frestelse layers of potato, onion and
    anchovies baked in cream
jordgubbar strawberries
jordärtskockspuré artichoke purée
järpe hazel-grouse
kalkon turkey
kallskuret cold meats
kalops beef stew served with beetroot
kalvbräss calves' sweetbreads
kalvfilé fillet of veal
kalvfricassé veal fricassee
kalvschnitzel veal cutlet
kalvsylta calves' brawn
kassler smoked tenderloin of pork

kavring pumpernickel *(type of bread)*
knäckebröd crispbread
kokt boiled, poached
kokt potatis boiled potatoes
kokt rimmad boiled in brine
kokt varmkorv boiled sausage
kolja haddock
korvgryta sausage casserole
korvkaka sausage and oatmeal pudding
kronärtskockor artichokes
kroppkakor potato dumplings filled with
    chopped pork
krusbär gooseberry
kräftor crayfish
kummel hake
kyckling chicken
kycklinglever chicken liver
kåldolmar cabbage rolls filled with minced
    beef and rice
kålpudding cabbage and minced beef pudding
    baked in the oven
kålrötter swedes
kålsoppa cabbage soup
köttbullar meat balls
köttfärslimpa minced beef loaf
köttgryta beef casserole
köttsoppa clear beef soup with vegetables
lammfricassé lamb fricassee
lammstek joint of lamb
lapskojs broth made of meat, vegetables and
    fish
lax salmon
legymsallad vegetable salad
leverbiff fried sliced liver
leverpastej liver pâté
lingon cowberry *(like cranberry)*
lussekatt 'Lucia' buns made with saffron
lutfisk dried cod, soaked in lye and cooked
lättöl low strength beer
lök onion

lövbiff sliced beef fried with onions
majskolvar corn on the cob
makaroner macaroni
marängsviss (hovdessert) meringue layered
  with whipped cream and melted plain
  chocolate
matjessill a type of salt herring
mellanöl medium strength beer
mesost sweet whey cheese
morötter carrots
mousserande fizzy
musslor mussels
njure kidney
nyponsoppa rose-hip soup
nässelsoppa nettle soup
olja oil
orre blackcock
oxfilé fillet of beef
oxrulader rolled beef with stuffing
oxstek joint of beef
palsternacka parsnip
pannbiff beefburgers
pannkakor pancakes
paprika green or red pepper
pepparrotskött boiled beef with horseradish
  sauce
plommon plum
plommonspäckad fläskkarré roast pork
  with prunes
potatismos mashed potatoes
potatissallad potato salad
prinskorv mini-sausages
purjolök leek
pyttipanna hash of meat, potato and onion
päron pear
pölsa hash made of meat and barley
rabarber rhubarb
rabarberkompott stewed rhubarb
raggmunkar potato pancakes
renstek joint of reindeer

revbensspjäll spare-ribs
rimmad skinka salt beef
ripa grouse
ris rice
ris à la Malta rice pudding served with
 whipped cream and jam
risgrynsgröt rice and milk porridge
 (*Christmas dish*)
rostbiff rare roast beef
rotmos mashed turnips
råbiff steak tartare
rådjursstek joint of roedeer
rågbröd rye bread
rårivna morötter grated carrots
räkor shrimps
räksallad shrimp salad
röda vinbär redcurrants
rödbeta beetroot
rödkål red cabbage
rödspätta plaice
rödvin red wine
rökt lax smoked salmon
rökt makrill smoked mackerel
rökt sik smoked char
saftkräm fruit purée thickened with potato
 flour
saltgurka salt gherkin
salt sill salt herring
sardiner sardines
schalottenlök shallot
semlor buns with marzipan and fresh cream
 (*eaten at Lent*)
senap mustard
senapssill salt herring in mustard sauce
sik whitefish
sill herring
sillbullar herring balls
sillgratäng herring au gratin
sillsallad herring salad
silltallrik selection of various herrings

sjömansbiff beef, onion and potato casseroled in beer
skinka ham
skorpor rusks
skånsk kryddsill Skåne spiced herring
slottsstek pot roast with anchovies, brandy and syrup
smultron wild strawberry
smör butter
smörgås sandwich
smörgåsbord cold buffet table
snaps potato-based liquor flavoured with herbs
sniglar snails
sparris asparagus
sparrissoppa cream of asparagus soup
spenat spinach
spenatsoppa spinach soup
starköl strong beer
stekt fried, roast
stekt falukorv fried pork sausage
stekt fläsk roast pork
stekt strömming fried Baltic herring
strömmingsflundror fillets of Baltic herring stuffed with parsley
strömmingslåda Baltic herring baked in milk with dill and onions
stuvad lake poached burbot in white sauce
stuvad potatis potatoes poached in white sauce
stuvad spenat spinach poached in white sauce
surströmming fermented Baltic herring
svampgratinerad oxfilé fillet of beef and mushrooms au gratin
svarta vinbär blackcurrants
syltomelett sweet omelette with jam
T-benstek T-bone steak
tjäder capercaillie *(type of grouse)*
tomat tomato
tomatsoppa cream of tomato soup
torsk cod

tranbär cranberry
tunga tongue
tårta gâteau
ugnsbakad skinka oven-baked ham
ugnskokt fiskfilé oven-baked fillet of fish
ugnspannkaka thick baked pancake
ugnsstekt revbensspjäll roast spare-ribs
varmrätt main course
vetebröd tea loaf
vinkokt cooked in wine
vitkål white cabbage
vitkålssallad white cabbage salad
vitlök garlic
vitt matbröd white bread
vitt vin white wine
våfflor waffles
västkustsallad west coast salad (*salad of shellfish*)
wienerbröd Danish pastry
wienerkorv frankfurter-style sausage
ål eel
ägg egg
äggröra scrambled eggs
älg elk
älgstek joint of elk
äppelmos apple purée
ärter peas
ärtsoppa yellow split pea soup
ättika vinegar
ättikssill soused herring
ättiksströmming soused Baltic herring
öl beer

ALTHOUGH the food of Switzerland has obvious similarities with that of Germany, France and Italy (see the sections on the food of these countries for useful phrases on ordering and a more extensive menu guide) there are many local unique specialities that are worth trying.

German Switzerland is particularly well-known for special types of sausage, smoked and dried meats, as is the canton of Vaud. You will find a variety of excellent cakes and pastries throughout Switzerland. French Switzerland is famous for **fondue**. Recipes vary from region to region, but the essential ingredients of a **fondue** are melted cheese and white wine, into which mixture you dip pieces of bread. In the canton of Valais, the speciality is **raclette**, large portions of melted cheese served with potatoes, ham and pickles. In Italian Switzerland, you will find a wide variety of pasta dishes. A traditional dish there is **busecca**, a soup made from tripe, which is a very old Ticino speciality.

You should take the opportunity to sample Swiss wine which is not generally available for export. Valais and Vaud are the main wine-producing areas. The Valais region is known for **Dole**, a red wine, but mainly for a variety of white wines: **Fendant**, a dry full wine, is the most famous, **Johannisberg** and **Hermitage**. If in Vaud, you should try **St Saphorin**, a dry fruity white wine and **Salvagnin** (red). Also worth sampling are Swiss spirits made from fruit, for example **Pflümli**, a liquor made from plums, and **Wiliamine** which is made from pears.

A service charge is included in restaurant bills in Switzerland so there is no need to leave a tip.

SWISS-GERMAN FOOD

AARGAU

Aargauer Rüblitorte carrot cake
Apfelchüchli apple tarts
Badener Chräbeli aniseed biscuits *(served at Christmas)*
Brotsuppe bread soup
Kartoffelpfluten potato dumplings with melted butter
Räbebappe turnip soup

APPENZELL

Appenzeller Biberfladen flat gingerbread with marzipan
Appenzeller Rahmfladen flat cream cake
Chäshappech fried cheese in batter
Hörnli (Teigwaren) mit Apfelmus macaroni with stewed apple
Mostbröckli dried beef
Rahmfladen flatcakes filled with cream or honey

BASEL

Basler Brunsli sweet chocolate biscuits *(served at Christmas)*
Basler Leckerli honey biscuits
Cervelat pork sausage
Lummerbraten roast fillet of beef
Mehlsuppe flour soup *(served at New Year and at Basle 'Fasnacht' carnival)*
Züblewäje onion pie *(served at New Year and at Basle 'Fasnacht' carnival)*

BERN

Bern Braid plait-shaped bread
Berner Herzen heart-shaped gingerbread

Berner Platte platter consisting of ham, bacon, sausage, beef and tongue, served with hot sauerkraut or beans
Emmental mild hard cheese with holes
Emmentaler Lammvoressen lamb stew
Rösti fried finely grated potatoes
Ziebelechüche onion pie *(served on fourth Monday in November in Old Town of Bern)*

GLARUS

Glarner Birnbrot pastry loaf with almonds, pears and nuts
Glarner Pastete pastry filled with various types of mushroom
Schabzieger small sticks of herb cheese

GRAUBÜNDEN

Birnbrot pastry loaf with almonds, pears and nuts
Bündnerfleisch air-dried beef
Bündner Gerstensuppe barley soup with smoked meat
Bündner Teller dried meats
Engadiner Nusstorte nut cake

LUZERN

Luzerner Chügelipastete pastry filled with meat balls
Luzerner Lebkuchen cake made with pear concentrate
Martinigans goose
Willisauer Ringli ring-shaped hard biscuits

SCHAFFHAUSEN

Gefüllte Zwiebeln stuffed onions
Grayling à la Schaffhausen grayling *(fish similar to salmon)* fried in butter

Kutteln nach Schaffhauser Art tripe
  Schaffhausen-style
Schaffhauser Katzenzüngli 'cat tongues',
  delicate hazelnut meringues
Schübling large spicy sausage

SCHWYZ

Gebrante Creme crème caramel
Gedämpftes Huhn steamed chicken
Kabissuppe cabbage soup
Käsesuppe cheese soup
Suu baggli baked ham shank
Suuri Gummeli potato slices in white sour
  sauce

SOLOTHURN

Leberspiess liver pieces on a skewer
Linsensuppe lentil soup
Weissrübensuppe white turnip soup

ST GALLEN

Apfelrösti fried bread with sliced apples
St Galler Bauerbratwurst type of sausage
St Galler Käsersuppe cheese soup
Schaffleisch mit Karotten mutton with
  carrots
St Galler Klostertorte monastery tart

THURGAU

Eglifilets Arenenberg fillets of perch
Gebratene Tauben fried pigeon
Gottlieber Hüppen delicate pastry rolls
Thurgauer Apfeltorte apple tart
Thurgauer Leberknödel liver dumplings
Thurgauer Schweinehals stewed neck of
  pork

UNTERWALDEN

Ländermagronen macaroni cooked in milk, mixed with diced potatoes, covered in cheese and baked, garnished with browned onions

Rindszunge und weiße Sauce beef tongue in white sauce

URI

Äeplermagronen macaroni cooked in milk then covered in cheese and baked, garnished with browned onions

Brischtner Bira dessert made with dried pears

Rys and Pohr type of risotto with leeks and garnished with browned onions

Urner Häfelichabis spicy lamb and cabbage stew

Urner Nusskuchen nutty cake

ZUG

Forellen Filets Zuger Art fillets of trout

Pastete vom Kalbfleisch veal in pastry

Röteli fish of the char family with reddish meat, braised with herbs and white wine

Zuger Kirschtorte gâteau flavoured with Kirsch *(liqueur made from wild cherries)*

ZÜRICH

Birchermüsli breakfast dish of oats, water, condensed milk, lemon juice, nuts and apples

Pfarrnaustorte Zurich vicarage gâteau

Rösti nach Zürcher Landfrauen Art finely grated potatoes with onions and diced bacon

Wollishofer Chnödelsuppe noodle soup

Züri Geschnätzlets finely sliced veal Zurich-style with thinly sliced calf's kidney in a mushroom, cream and white wine sauce

SWISS-FRENCH FOOD

FRIBOURG

beignets de bénichon deep-fried sweet cakes
sprinkled with icing sugar

fondue fribourgeoise au vacherin fondue
made of melted vacherin cheese, water and
flavoured with kirsch, garlic and nutmeg

fondue moitié-moitié fondue of melted
vacherin and gruyère cheese, white wine,
kirsch and sometimes garlic

gruyère spicy hard cheese *(often quite salty)*

petits ramequins à la fribourgeoise small
bread and cheese tarts

ragoût d'agneau aux raisins lamb stew
cooked in wine with sultanas and flavoured
with cloves

soupe au vin vegetable soup made with red
wine and chicken stock

vacherin fribourgeois creamy mild cheese

GENEVE

cardons au gratin dish of cardoons *(a prickly
vegetable similar to artichoke)* covered in
creamy white sauce topped with grated cheese
and browned in the oven

filets de perches St Saphorin fillets of perch
cooked in dry white wine

fricassée de porc genevoise Geneva-style
pork fricassee

longeolles seasonal *(autumn/winter)* pork
sausage spiced with caraway and typical of
Geneva

malakoffs cheese dipped in batter and deep-
fried

omble chevalier char *(fish)* from Lake Geneva
served in a white wine and butter sauce

soupe à l'oignon onion soup made with wine,
  sometimes poured over toasted bread and
  cheese and then browned in the oven
soupe à l'oseille sorrel soup
tarte aux fruits frangipane tart with fruit
  arranged on a layer of custard containing
  ground almonds
tuiles aux amandes almond biscuits

JURA

civet de lapin/lièvre de Tante Jeanne
  marinaded rabbit/hare stew
escargots à la mode ajoulette snails served
  in their shells with a butter sauce flavoured
  with shallots, garlic, nutmeg, herbs, paprika,
  parmesan and lemon juice
marinade de porc à la jurassienne
  marinaded pork stewed with vegetables
omelette jurassienne mushroom omelette
truites du Doubs trout from the river Doubs,
  grilled and served with melted butter
truites jurassiennes farcies trout stuffed
  with fish and bread, served with mushrooms

NEUCHATEL

chou farci à la neuchâteloise cabbage
  stuffed with a mixture of pork, veal and ham
fondue neuchâteloise fondue made with
  melted gruyère and emmental cheese, white
  wine, kirsch and garlic
saucisses Château de Colombier regional
  sausage wrapped in ham and puff pastry
tripes à la neuchâteloise dish of braised
  tripe and vegetables served with a white sauce

VALAIS

chevreuil aux châtaignes marinaded venison
  stewed with chestnuts

flan aux abricots shallow dish of apricots
stewed in an egg and cream custard

gâteau aux myrtilles bilberry tart

**pommes de terre au fromage à la
valaisanne** diced potatoes prepared in white
wine sauce, over which thin slices of cheese are
allowed to melt just before serving

potée valaisanne dish of vegetables, potatoes,
smoked sausage and bacon, simmered together
in wine and stock, eaten with stewed dried
pears

raclette melted cheese served with boiled
potatoes, smoked ham and pickles (a large
piece of cheese is placed in front of an open
fire, or a custom-built electric fire, and when it
melts, large scrapings are dropped onto plates
— the diner usually receives more than one
serving)

rizotto au saffran risotto with smoked bacon,
cooked ham, tomatoes and flavoured with
saffron, garlic and thyme

tarte aux asperges savoury flan with
asparagus and ham, topped with cheese

**tranches valaisannes aux
fraises** strawberry mousse flan decorated
with fresh strawberries

truite du bisse trout baked in local white
wine, with a fir tree bud in its mouth for
decoration and flavouring

viande séchée du Valais dried raw meat

VAUD

carottes au lard sticks of carrot, bacon and
onion simmered together and served in a sauce

crêpes du Pays d'en Haut gruyère cheese
pancakes

fricassée à la vaudoise pork, pig's trotter
and vegetable stew, flavoured with white wine,
coriander and herbs

gratin vaudois et saucisson fumé layered
  potatoes and cheese dish with white wine and
  cream, on top of which a local smoked sausage
  has been cooked *(served with cabbage salad)*
papet de poireaux et saucisse de foie local
  liver sausage served on top of a mound of
  potatoes and leeks mashed together
perches à la nyonnaise perch served with a
  white wine sauce, ground hazelnuts and
  croûtons
soupe au chou cabbage, bacon and potato
  soup
tarte au vin vaudoise tart filled with
  caramelized sugar and white wine

SWISS-ITALIAN FOOD

TICINO

busecca tripe and vegetable soup
coniglio alla ticinese rabbit Ticino-style
formaggini small cheeses made from goat's
  milk, often served with oil, vinegar and pepper
manzo brasato roast beef with rich red wine
  sauce
risotto ai funghi rice dish made with
  tomatoes and dried mushrooms
zabaglione dessert made from egg yolks,
  sugar, wine and brandy

IN Turkey, there are eating places to suit every budget. You can eat cheaply at a **pideci**, a **köfteci** or **kebapçi** (kebab house). A **pideci** specializes in making **pide** *[peedeh]*, a kind of pitta bread with different toppings, and a **köfteci** serves meat balls. At some open-air restaurants one can select and cook one's own meat on a charcoal grill.

If you want a simple and cheap meal, go to an **içkisiz lokanta**. This type of restaurant opens at 7 a.m. and closes early at about 9.30 p.m. Breakfast can be soup, **sahlep** (a spicy milk drink with cinnamon), milk or yogurt. For lunch and dinner, meat or vegetable dishes are available. These are usually cooked beforehand and displayed at the front of the establishment and — as there may not be a menu — you usually order by indicating the dishes of your choice to the waiter. Alcohol is not served in an **içkisiz lokanta**, but you can buy soft drinks, fruit juice, **ayran** (a yogurt drink) or mineral water.

For a more elaborate meal, try an **içkili lokanta** — a more formal licensed restaurant. Here, a wide variety of hors d'oeuvres are served with drinks. The most popular drink is **rakı**, usually accompanied by a glass of iced water to mix with it. Turks make imaginative use of many vegetables such as aubergines, courgettes, peppers, and beans, and in coastal areas, fish. If you are on the coast or in a large city like Ankara, you should visit a **balık lokantasi** — a restaurant specialising in fresh seafood and hors d'oeuvres. Pork is available only in a few luxury restaurants in big cities and, as it is not eaten by Muslims, it is not tactful to ask for it.

Whether the bill includes a service charge or not is indicated on the menu. The charge is usually 10-15%, but you are still expected to leave a 10% tip for the waiter.

ORDERING

excuse me . . .!
bakar mısınız!
[bakar muh-suh-nuhz]

can I order please?
yemek siparişimi verebilir miyim?
[yemek seepareesheemee verebeeleer meeyeem]

one . . ./two . . .
bir . . ./iki . . .
[beer/eekee]

that's for me/him
o bana/ona
[o bana/ona]

can I see the menu again?
yemek listesini tekrar görebilir miyim?
[yemek leesteseenee tekrar gurebeeleer meeyeem]

can you bring me another red wine/beer?
Bana bir kırmızı şarap/bira daha getirir misiniz?
[bana beer kuhrmuhzuh sharap/bcera da-ha geteereer meeseeneez]

could I have the bill please?
hesabı getirir misiniz, lütfen?
[hesabuh geteereer meeseeneez, lewtfen]

if the waiter/waitress says:
  afiyet olsun!
  [afee-yet olsoon]
  hope you enjoyed your meal

you could reply:
  teşekkür ederim
  [teshek-kewr edereem]
  yes, thank you

SOME BASIC WORDS

beer bir bira *[beer beera]*
bottle bir şişe *[beer sheesheh]*
brandy bir konyak
bread ekmek *[ekmek]*
coffee kahve *[kah-veh]*
cup bir fincan *[beer feenjan]*
dry sek
fork bir çatal *[beer chatal]*
fruit juice bir meyva suyu *[beer mayva sooyoo]*
gin and tonic bir cin-tonik *[beer jeen-toneek]*
glass bir bardak *[beer bardak]*
half-bottle bir yarım şişe *[beer yaruhm sheesheh]*
hot chocolate bir kakao *[beer kakao]*
ice buz *[booz]*
knife bir bıçak *[beer buhchak]*
lager bir bira *[beer beera]*
lemonade bir gazoz *[beer gazoz]*
milk süt *[sewt]*
mineral water maden suyu *[maden soo-yoo]*
mineral water (fizzy) gazlı maden suyu *[gazluh maden soo-yoo]*
napkin bir peçete *[beer pecheteh]*
orange juice bir portakal suyu *[beer portakal soo-yoo]*
pepper karabiber *[karabeeber]*
red wine kırmızı şarap *[kuhrmuhzuh sharap]*
rosé wine pembe şarap *[pembeh sharap]*
salt tuz *[tooz]*
spoon bir kaşık *[beer kashuhk]*
sugar şeker *[sheker]*
sweet tatlı *[tatluh]*
tea çay *[chı]*
water su *[soo]*
whisky bir viski *[beer veeskee]*
white wine beyaz şarap *[bayaz sharap]*

UNDERSTANDING THE MENU

Adana kebabı spicy meatballs
alabalık trout
Arnavut ciğeri 'Albanian' spicy fried liver
 with onions
aşure 'Noah's pudding' — a dessert made
 from wheat grains, nuts and dried fruit
ayran drinking yogurt
ayva laabı quince jelly
badem kurabiyesi almond cakes
badempare almond cakes in syrup
bakla broad beans
baklava pastry filled with nuts and syrup
balık buğulaması fish baked with tomatoes
balık pilaki fish baked with potatoes, carrots,
 celery and onions
bamya okra, ladies fingers
barbunya red mullet
barbunya pilakisi dried beans cooked in olive
 oil *(served hot or cold)*
barbunya tava fried red mullet
bazlama unleavened bread cooked on a hot-
 plate
beyaz peynir white cheese
beyaz şarap white wine
beyin salatası brain salad
beyin tava brain slices in batter
biftek steak
biber dolması stuffed green peppers
bira beer
boza thick fermented grain drink
böbrek ızgara grilled kidneys
börek layered pastry with various fillings
buğulama steamed, poached
bulgur pilavı cracked wheat cooked with
 tomatoes
Bursa kebabı grilled lamb on pitta bread with
 yogurt and tomato sauce
bülbül yuvası dessert with nuts and syrup

cacık cucumber in garlic-flavoured yogurt
ciğer sarması minced liver wrapped in lamb's
fat
ciğer tava fried liver
Çerkez tavuğu Circassian cold chicken in
walnut and garlic sauce
çılbır poached eggs with yogurt
çiğ köfte raw meatballs made of minced meat,
pounded wheat and chilli powder
çikolatalı pasta chocolate cake
çilekli dondurma strawberry ice cream
çips crisps
çiroz salted dried mackerel
çoban salatası salad of tomatoes, peppers,
cucumbers and onion
çorba soup
çöp kebabı small pieces of lamb baked on
wooden spits
dana rozbif roast veal
dil ox tongue
dil balığı sole
dilber dudağı sweet pastry with nut filling
dolma stuffed vegetables *(with or without meat)*
domates salatası tomato salad
domates salçalı patlıcan kızartması fried
aubergines with tomato and garlic sauce
dondurma ice cream
döner kebab lamb grilled on a spit and served
in thin slices *(served with rice and salad)*
düğün çorbası 'wedding' soup made of meat
stock, yogurt and egg
ekmek bread
ekmek kadayıfı sweet pastry
elma suyu apple juice
elma tatlısı apple dessert
enginar artichokes
etli Ayşe kadın meat with green beans
etli bezelye pea and meat stew
etli biber dolması peppers stuffed with rice
and meat

etli domates dolması tomatoes stuffed with rice and meat

etli kuru fasulye lamb and haricot beans in tomato sauce

etli lahana dolması cabbage leaves stuffed with rice and meat

etli yaprak dolması vine leaves stuffed with rice and meat

ezo gelin çorbası lentil and rice soup

fasulye pilaki beans in olive oil

fasulye piyazı bean and onion salad

fava broad bean purée

fırın baked, oven-roasted

fıstıklı with pistachio nuts

gazoz fizzy drink

güllaç rice wafers stuffed with nuts and cooked in rose-flavoured milky syrup

gümüş balığı silverfish

güveç meat and vegetable stew

hamsi anchovy

hanım parmağı 'lady's fingers' — finger-shaped pastry sticks in syrup

hardal mustard

haşlanmış yumurta boiled egg

havuç salatası shredded carrot salad

helva general name for various sweets made from cereals, nuts, sesame oil and honey

hoşaf stewed fruit

hünkar beğendi 'sultan's delight' — lamb served with aubergine purée

ıhlamur lime blossom tea

ıspanaklı börek spinach wrapped in pastry

ıspanaklı yumurta eggs with spinach

ızgara balık grilled fish

ızgara köfte grilled meatballs

içecek beverage

içki alcoholic drink

içli köfte meatballs stuffed with cracked wheat

iç pilav rice with currants, pine nuts and onions

imam bayıldı split aubergine with tomatoes and onions *(eaten cold)*
irmik helvası semolina helva
İskender kebabı grilled lamb on pitta bread with tomato sauce and yogurt
islim kebabı steamed kebab
istakoz lobster
istiridye oysters
işkembe çorbası tripe soup
kabak dolması stuffed courgettes
kabak kızartması fried marrows
kabak tatlısı pumpkin with syrup and walnuts
kadın budu köfte 'lady's thighs' — meat and rice croquettes
kadın göbeği 'lady's navel' — a ring-shaped syrupy pastry
kağıtta pişmiş baked in paper
kalkan turbot
karagöz black bream
karışık ızgara mixed grill
karides prawns
karides tavası prawns fried in batter
karnıbahar tavası fried cauliflower
karnıyarık split aubergine with meat filling
karpuz water melon
kavun honeydew melon
kaymaklı with clotted cream
kaymaklı dondurma dairy ice cream
kazan dibi pudding with a caramel base
kebap roast meat
kefal grey mullet
kereviz celery
kestane şekeri candied chestnuts
keşkek lamb with wheat
keşkül almond pudding
kılıç ızgara grilled swordfish
kılıç şiş swordfish on a skewer
kırmızı mercimek çorbası red lentil soup
kırmızı şarap red wine

kısır cracked wheat and paprika
kıymalı pide pitta bread with meat filling
kızarmış ekmek toast
kiraz cherries
koç yumurtası 'ram's eggs' — a delicacy made
   from ram's testicles
kokoreç lamb's intestines grilled on a spit
komposto cold stewed fruit
köfte meat balls or patties
kremalı pasta cream cake
kurabiye cake with almonds or other nuts
kuru fasulye haricot beans in tomato sauce
kuru köfte fried meatballs
kuskus pilavı couscous — cooked semolina,
   served with meat
kuşkonmaz asparagus
kuzu fırında roast leg of lamb
kuzu kapama lamb with lettuce
kuzu pirzolası grilled lamb chops
lahana dolması stuffed cabbage leaves
lahana turşusu pickled cabbage
lahmacun pancakes with spicy meat
levrek sea bass
limonata still lemon drink
lokum Turkish Delight
lüfer bluefish
makarna macaroni, noodles
mantar mushrooms
mantı type of ravioli
mayonezli balık fish with mayonnaise
menemen omelette with tomatoes and peppers
mercan bream
mercimek çorbası lentil soup
mersin balığı sturgeon
meşrubat soft drinks
midye dolması stuffed mussels
midye pilakisi mussels cooked in oil with
   vegetables
midye tavası fried mussels
muhallebi rice flour and rosewater pudding

muska böreği triangles of pastry filled with cheese and parsley
mücver vegetable patties
nemse böreği meat pie with puff pastry
nohutlu yahni lamb and chickpeas
orman kebabı veal or lamb first fried then cooked with vegetables
paça çorbası soup made from lamb's trotters
palamut tunny
pancar turşusu pickled beetroot
pastırma cummin and garlic cured beef
pastırmalı yumurta fried eggs with 'pastırma'
patates köftesi potato and cheese balls
patates kızartması chips
patates püresi creamed potatoes
patates salatası potato salad
patlıcan kebabı aubergine wrapped around pieces of meat and roasted
patlıcanlı pilav rice with aubergines
patlıcan salatası aubergine dip
pavurya crab
pembe şarap rosé wine
peynirli omlet cheese omelette
peynirli pide cheese pitta bread
peynir tatlısı small cheese cakes in syrup
pırasa leek
pide pitta bread
pilaki white bean salad
piliç chicken
piliç ızgarası grilled chicken
pirzola lamb chops
pisi balığı plaice
piyaz haricot bean salad
poğaça pastries with meat or cheese filling
portakal suyu orange juice
puf böreği meat or cheese pasties
rafadan yumurta soft-boiled egg
rakı Turkish national drink, distilled from grape juice and aniseed-flavoured
reçel jam

revani sweet semolina pastry
roka kind of watercress
rosto roasted
rus salatası Russian salad made from
vegetables and mayonnaise
sahanda yumurta fried eggs
sahlep drink made from 'sahlep' root in hot
milk and cinnamon
salata salad
salçalı köfte meatballs in tomato sauce
saray lokması fried batter dipped in syrup
sardalya sardines
sarığı burma 'twisted turban' — turban-
shaped 'baklava'
sazan carp
sebze çorbası vegetable soup
semizotu purslane *(herb)*
sigara böreği cigarette-shaped fried pastry
filled with cheese and parsley
simit ring-shaped bread covered with sesame
seeds
som balığı salmon
sosis sausage
su böreği layered pastry
sucuk Turkish sausage with spices and garlic
su muhallebisi rice flour pudding with
rosewater
supanglez chocolate pudding
sütlaç rice pudding
şalgam turnip
şehriye çorbası vermicelli soup with lemon
şehriyeli pilav pilaff with vermicelli
şekerpare small cakes with syrup
şerbet sweetened and iced fruit juices
şıra grape juice
şiş kebabı small pieces of lamb grilled on
skewers
şiş köfte grilled meatballs on skewers
talaş kebabı lamb baked in pastry
tarama fish roe dip

taratorlu karnıbahar cauliflower with nut
  and garlic sauce
tarhana çorbası traditional soup with dried
  yogurt, tomato and pimento
tas kebabı diced lamb with rice
tatar böreği ravioli
tatlı sweet dessert
tavuk chicken
tavuk göğsü 'chicken breast pudding' — a
  creamy dessert made with rice flour and finely
  shredded chicken
tel kadayıfı shredded wheat stuffed with nuts
  in syrup
terbiyeli köfte meatballs with egg and lemon
  juice
torik large tunny
tost toasted sandwich
tulumba tatlısı semolina doughnut in syrup
turşu pickled vegetables
tükenmez eggs fried with tomatoes and sweet
  peppers
türlü meat and vegetable stew
un helvası flour helva
uskumru dolması stuffed mackerel
üzüm grapes
vişne suyu black cherry juice
yahni meat stew with onions
yaprak dolması stuffed vine leaves
yayla çorbası yogurt soup
yengeç crab
yeşil salata green salad
yoğurtlu kebap kebab with pitta bread and
  yogurt
yoğurt tatlısı yogurt cake in syrup
zerde saffron rice dessert
zeytin olives
zeytinyağlı enginar artichokes in olive oil
zeytinyağlı pırasa leeks in olive oil
zeytinyağlı yaprak dolması vine leaves
  stuffed with rice, pine nuts and raisins

YUGOSLAVIAN FOOD

THE most pleasant eating places in the warm months are garden restaurants (often with a beautiful view) which open for lunch and tend to remain open until late at night. Grilled meats are particularly good. Privately-owned local restaurants in small towns and villages are often superb. If away from the big cities or tourist centres, ask for local specialities (**lokalni specijaliteti** *[lokalnee spetsee-yaleetetee]*). If you are on the coast, ask for the day's catch, **sveža riba** *[svezha reeba]*.

You should take the opportunity to sample Yugoslavian national dishes: **musaka**, Hungarian-style **gulaš** and **paprikaš** (stew made with meat, vegetables and paprika); **pasulj** (beans or lentils with smoked meat); **sarma** (stuffed cabbage leaves); **đuveč** (a casserole of meat, rice and summer vegetables); **čorba** or **juha** (soups); and **pita** (a savoury or sweet pie).

Veal is always very good and tender. Sucking pig and lamb roasts can be excellent. These are ordered by the kilo and served with chopped onion and bread. However, if you want a good beefsteak, order **biftek** (Serbo-Croatian for tender steak). Otherwise beef is best eaten in stews such as **gulaš**.

Yugoslavia produces several unique brandies — try the traditional plum brandy, **šljivovica**, or the herb brandy, **travarica**.

ORDERING

waiter/waitress!
konobar/konobarice!
[konobar/konobareetseh]

can I order, please?
mogu li da poručim?
[mogoo lee da poroocheem]

one . . ./two . . .
jedanput . . ./dvaput . . .
[yedanput/dvaput]

that's for me/him
to je za mene/njega
[toh yeh za meneh/nyega]

can I see the menu again?
molim vas, donesite mi opet jelovnik
[moleem vas doneseet-eh mee opet yelovneek]

can you bring me another red wine/beer?
molim vas, donesite me još jedno crno vino/pivo
[moleem vas doneseet-eh mee yosh yedno tsurno veeno/peevo]

could I have the bill please?
molim vas, donesite mi račun
[moleem vas doneseet-eh mee rachoon]

if the waiter/waitress says:
  da li je sve bilo u redu?
  [da lee yeh sveh beelo oo redoo]
  was everything all right?

you can reply:
  jeste, hvala!
  [yest-eh hvala]
  it was very nice, thank you!

SOME BASIC WORDS

(When two words are given, *(S)* indicates the Serbian and *(C)* the Croatian.)

beer pivo *[peevo]*
bottle boca *[botsa]*
brandy (French) konjak *[konyak]*
brandy (Yugoslavian) rakija *[rakee-ya]*

....

bread *(C)*kruh/*(S)*hleb *[krooн/нlyeb]*
coffee kava *[ka̱va]*
cup *(C)*šalica/*(S)*šolja *[sha̱leetsa/sho̱lya]*
dry suho *[sooнo̱]*
fork viljuška *[ve̱elyooshka]*
fruit juice voćni sok *[vochnee sok]*
glass čaša *[cha̱sha]*
gin and tonic džin i tonic *[jeen ee to̱neek]*
half-bottle mala boca *[ma̱la bo̱tsa]*
hot chocolate kakao *[ka̱ka-o]*
ice led
knife nož *[noj]*
lager lager
lemonade limunada *[leemoona̱da]*
milk mlijeko *[mleeye̱ko]*
mineral water *(fizzy)* mineralna voda
  [me̱eneralna vo̱da]
napkin salveta *[salve̱ta]*
orange juice sok od narandže *[sok od
  na̱ranjeh]*
pepper biber *[be̱eber]*
red wine crno vino *[tsu̱rno ve̱eno]*
rosé ružica *[roo̱jeetsa]*
salt *(S)*so/*(C)*sol
spoon *(S)*kašika/*(C)*žlica *[ka̱sheeka/jle̱etsa]*
sugar šećer *[she̱cher]*
sweet slatko *[sla̱tko]*
tea čaj *[chɪ]*
water voda *[vo̱da]*
whisky viski
white wine bijelo vino *[be̱e-yelo ve̱eno]*

UNDERSTANDING THE MENU

ajvar hors-d'oeuvre made from aubergine and
  peppers
alaska čorba rich spicy fish stew served with
  fried bread
apatinski paprikaš Apatin fish stew with
  onions, peppers, chillis, tomatoes and wine

bademi almonds
baklava thin layers of sweet flaky pastry filled
  with ground walnuts
barbun red mullet
baren boiled
batak drumstick
bečki odrezak breaded veal cutlet
beli white
bešamel white sauce
bijela kafa white coffee
bijeli white
bijeli bubrezi sweetbreads
bijeli luk garlic
bijeli sir feta cheese
bijelo meso breast *(poultry)*
bijelo vino white wine
blitva mangold greens *(type of beet)*
boranija French beans
borovnice blackcurrants
bosanski lonac Bosnian hot-pot
bravetina mutton
breskve peaches
brizle sweetbreads
brodet na dalmatinski način Dalmatian fish
  stew with onions, tomatoes, wine and Tabasco
bubrezi kidneys
bujon meat stock
bundeva pumpkin
burek minced meat or cheese pie made with
  flaky pastry
but leg
buter butter
cipal grey mullet
crni hljeb wholemeal bread
crna kafa black Turkish coffee
crni luk onion
crno vino red wine
crveno vino rosé wine
cvekla beetroot
čaj tea

češnjak garlic
čorba od ... (thickened) soup made of ...
čorbast pasulj bean soup
ćevapčići grilled minced meat finger rolls
ćufteta meat balls
ćulbastija grilled slice of well-matured best rib of beef
ćuretina turkey meat
ćurka na podvarku turkey with sauerkraut
dagnje mussels
dimljen smoked
dinja melon
divljač game
dobro pečen well-done
dolma stuffed vegetables
domaći home-made
dunja quince
džem od ... ... jam
džem od šipaka rosehip jam
džigerica na žaru grilled liver
đuveč meat, rice and vegetable casserole
engleski čaj English tea
faširane šnicle large fried meatballs
fazan pheasant
feferoni hot chillies
flekice small square-shaped pasta
gibanica layered cheese and egg pie
girica pickerel *(whitebait)*
glavno jelo main course
gljive mushrooms
govedina 1. beef; 2. meat
govedski/goveđi ... beef ...
grah beans
grašak peas
grožđe grapes
grožđice raisins
gulaš stew, goulash *(Hungarian style)*
guska goose
guščetina goose meat
guščija jetra goose liver

guščiji ... goose ...
hladan cold
hladno predjelo cold hors-d'oeuvre
hleb/hljeb bread
hren horseradish
hrenovke frankfurters, hot-dogs
integralna riža brown rice
istarski brodet Istrian spicy fish stew
jabuke apples
jabuke u šlafroku sliced apples coated in
  sweet batter and fried
jagnjeća kapama braised lamb with spinach
jagnjeći perkelt stew made from lamb and
  peppers
jagnjetina lamb
jagode strawberries
jaja u aspiku eggs in aspic
jaja u majonezu eggs mayonnaise
jaje egg
jaje na oko fried egg
janjeći ... lamb ...
janjetina lamb
jastog lobster
jegulja eel
jelo 1. dish; 2. food
jelovnik menu
jesetra sturgeon
jetra liver
jezik tongue
jogurt drinking yoghurt
juha soup
junetina young beef
kačamak polenta *(a cornmeal soup or dumpling
  eaten with meat or milk)*
kačkavalj hard full-fat cheese
kadaif dessert similar to shredded wheat with
  honey
kajgana scrambled eggs
kajmak a rich cream cheese
kajsije apricots

kajsijevača apricot brandy
kalja dish made of cabbage, onion and meat
kamenice sa limunom oysters with lemon
kamilica/kamomila camomile tea
karabatak thigh *(poultry)*
karfiol cauliflower
kasato ice cream with candied fruit
kaštradina smoked mutton cooked with
  cabbage, potatoes and beans
kečiga sterlet *(fish)*
kelj savoy cabbage, kale
kesten pire chestnut purée
kiflice filled sweet croissants
kikiriki peanuts
kisela pavlaka sour cream
kisele paprike pickled peppers
kiseli krastavci pickled gherkins
kiselo mleko/mlijeko Greek-style yogurt
kiselo vrhnje sour cream
klekovača plum brandy with juniper
knedle od sira cheese dumplings
knedle sa šljivama plum dumplings
kobasica sausage
komovica grape brandy
kompot od . . . stewed . . . *(fruit)*
kotlet chop
krastavac cucumber
krem-karamel crème caramel
krempita custard slice
krem supa od . . . cream of . . . soup
krmenadla chop
krofne doughnuts
krompir potatoes
krompir pire mashed potatoes
kruh bread
kruške pears
kruškovača pear brandy
krvav rare
krvavica black pudding
kuhan boiled

kupine blackberries
kupus cabbage
kuvan boiled
leća lentils
lepinja type of pitta bread
leskovačka mućkalica pork escalope with onions and hot peppers
lignja squid
limun lemon
list sole
lješnici/lješnjaci hazelnuts
losos salmon
lovački đuveč hunter's stew
loza/lozovača grape brandy
lubenica watermelon
mahune French beans
mak poppy seed
makovnjača poppy seed strudel
maline raspberries
marelice apricots
mariniran marinated
marmelada jam
maslac butter
masline olives
maslinovo ulje olive oil
mast pork fat, lard
med honey
meko kuhano jaje soft-boiled egg
miješana salata mixed salad
mileram sour cream
mladi grašak tender young peas
mladi krompir new potatoes
mladi sir fresh white cheese
mleko/mlijeko milk
mljeveno meso minced meat
morski račići 1. shrimps; 2. prawns
morski rakovi lobster
mozak brains
mrkva carrot
musaka od karfiola cauliflower moussaka

....

mušule mussels
na buteru sautéed in butter
nadeven stuffed
na gradele grilled
na kajmaku grilled on rich creamy cheese
narandža orange
naravni omlet plain omelette
na ražnju spit-roasted
na roštilju barbecued, grilled
na ulju cooked in oil
na žaru grilled
noklice plain dumplings
nudle dumplings
odrezak steak
ohridska pastrmka Lake Ohrid trout
omlet sa . . . . . . omelette
omlet sa šunkom ham omelette
orasi walnuts
oslić hake
ovčetina mutton
ovčiji sir cheese made from sheep's milk
ovseni hljeb/kruh oatmeal bread
palačinke sa . . . pancakes with . . .
palenta polenta *(a cornmeal soup or dumpling
    eaten with meat or milk)*
papazjanija beef and vegetable stew
paprikaš meat and vegetable stew flavoured
    with paprika
paprike red or green peppers
paradajz tomato
pariska šnicla/pariski odrezak veal steak
    in thin batter
pašteta pâté
pasticada Dalmatian beef stew with prunes
pastrmka trout
pasulj beans
pasulj bez mesa bean soup or stew without
    meat
paški sir hard, dry cheese
patka duck

pavlaka cream
pecivo roll, bun
pečen ... roast ...
pečurke mushrooms
pekmez od šipaka rosehip jam
peršun parsley
piće drink
pihtije/piktije aspic
pilav pilaff rice
pile chicken
pileći ... chicken ...
piletina chicken meat
pire od ... mashed, puréed ...
pirinač rice
pirjan braised
pita pie made with layers of thin flaky pastry
  with sweet or savoury fillings
pivo beer
plavi patlidžan aubergine
pljeskavica s lukom spicy beefburger with
  onions
pogača type of flat, round bread
pogačice sa čvarcima flat flaky buns with
  crackling
pohovan dipped in flour, egg and breadcrumbs
  and fried
pomfrit chips, French fries
poriluk leeks
poširana jaja poached eggs
potaž cream of vegetable soup
povrće vegetables
prasetina sucking pig
prebranac baked beans with onion
predjela hors d'oeuvres
proja corn bread
prokulice Brussels sprouts
prstaci small mussels
pršut smoked ham
pržen fried
pržen hljeb croûtons

pšenični hljeb wheat bread
punjen stuffed
pura polenta *(a cornmeal soup or dumpling eaten with meat or milk)*
pura/puran/purica turkey
puslice small meringues
raca duck
rajčica tomato
rak lobster
rakija brandy
rakovica crab
ražan/ražev kruh rye bread
ražnjići kebab
rebra ribs
ren horseradish
restovan sautéed with onions
rezanci noodles, tagliatelle
rezanci za juhu/supu thin egg noodles *(used in soups)*
riba fish
ribizle redcurrants
riblji . . . fish . . .
ringlice anchovy fillets
rizi-bizi rice with peas
rizoto risotto
riža rice
rolat od oraha walnut roll
rolat sa šunkom ham roll
roštilj grilled, barbecued
rotkvice radishes
rozbratna T-bone steak
ruska salata Russian salad
salata od . . . . . . salad
sardele anchovies
sarma cabbage leaves stuffed with mince and rice
sarma od kiselog kupusa stuffed soured cabbage leaves
sarma od vinovog lišća stuffed vine leaves
sa šećerom with sugar

sataraš stew made of onions, tomatoes,
  peppers and eggs
savijača strudel, turnover
sipa cuttlefish
sir cheese
sirće vinegar
skuša mackerel
slačica mustard
sladak . . . sweet . . .
sladoled od . . . . . . ice cream
slanina bacon
slani štapići savoury sticks
slatko od . . . 1. . . . in syrup; 2. . . . preserve
smokve figs
smuđ perch
sočivo lentils
soja soya beans
sok od naranče orange juice
som catfish
somun type of pitta bread
sos sauce
spanać spinach
srnetina venison
srpska salata Serbian salad
stono vino table wine
suho vino dry wine
sulc 1. jelly; 2. aspic
suncokretno ulje sunflower oil
supa od . . . . . . soup
sutlijaš rice pudding
suvo grožđe raisins
svinjetina pork
svinjski . . . pork
šampanj/šampanjac champagne
šampita squares of soft meringue in flaky
  pastry
šaran perch
šargarepe carrots
šatobrijan za dve/dvije osobe chateaubriand
  steak for two persons

šlag whipped cream
šljive plums
šljivovica plum brandy
šnenokle floating islands *(poached whisked egg white on top of custard)*
šnicla steak, cutlet
šopska salata mixed salad with feta cheese
španat spinach
šparga asparagus
štanglice od . . . dessert sticks made of . . .
štrudla od . . . . . . strudel
štuka pike
šumske jagode wild strawberries
šunka ham
tarator cucumber salad with sour cream
tašci/taške ravioli
teleći . . . veal . . .
teleći medaljon fillet of veal
teleći ragu veal ragoût
teletina veal
tikva 1. marrow; 2. pumpkin
tikvice courgettes
torta gâteau
trapist cheese similar to Port Salut
travnički sir white sheep's cheese
trešnje cherries
tučeno vrhnje whipped cream
tuna/tunj/tunjevina tuna
turska kava Turkish coffee
turšija pickled foods
tvrdo bareno jaje hard-boiled egg
urmašice finger-shaped cakes in syrup
valjušci dumplings
vino wine
višnje morello cherries
voće fruit
voćna salata fruit salad
vrhnje cream
zakuska mixed starter *(cold meat, cheese)*
zec/zečevina 1. hare; 2. rabbit

zelena salata lettuce, green salad
zeljanica spinach pie
zemička roll; bun
zubatac dentex *(fish)*